The Collected Poems of
ANDREW YOUNG

THE

COLLECTED POEMS

OF

# ANDREW YOUNG

ARRANGED WITH A

BIBLIOGRAPHICAL NOTE BY

LEONARD CLARK

---

WOOD-ENGRAVINGS BY

JOAN HASSALL

RUPERT HART-DAVIS

SOHO SQUARE LONDON

1960

PR6047
.O46 A6
1960

PRINTED IN GREAT BRITAIN
BY WESTERN PRINTING SERVICES LTD. BRISTOL

# Contents

5

7

9

10

11

# Bibliographical Note

ANDREW YOUNG'S first book of poems, *Songs of Night* (de la More Press) was published in 1910. Of that youthful collection, one poem only, 'The Leaf', has been retained in the present volume. There followed *Boaz and Ruth and Other Poems* (1920), *The Death of Eli and Other Poems* (1921), *Thirty-One Poems* (1922), *The Adversary* (1923), *The Bird-Cage* (1926), *The Cuckoo Clock* (1929) and *The New Shepherd* (1931). All these books, some merely pamphlets, were published in very small editions by John G. Wilson, up to and including 1923, and, after that date, by J. and E. Bumpus Ltd., and are all rare. Andrew Young became known to a wider public in 1933 with the publication of *Winter Harvest* (The Nonesuch Press).

*Winter Harvest* contained one poem, 'The Stars' from *Thirty-One Poems*, five, 'The Yellow Hammers', 'Late Autumn', 'The Last Leaf', 'The Flood', 'The Lane' from *The Bird-Cage*, two, 'In Romsey Abbey', 'The Old Tree' from *The Cuckoo Clock*, seven, 'March Hare', 'On the Pilgrims' Road', 'The Green Woodpecker', 'The Star', 'Loch Brandy', 'The Signpost', 'The Pines' from *The New Shepherd*, and thirteen revised poems which had appeared previously in the 'Wilson' books. The revised poems were 'In Moonlight' from *Thirty-One Poems*, 'The Beech', 'The Evening Star', 'The Spider', 'The Feather', 'The Wood', 'The Rain' from *The Bird-Cage*, 'Loch Luichart' and 'The Roman Wall' from *The Cuckoo Clock*, and 'Winter Morning', 'The Shadow', 'Autumn' and 'Illic Jacet' from *The New Shepherd*. *Winter Harvest* contained forty-five poems, of which seventeen were published in book form for the first time.

Andrew Young's next book of poems, *The White Blackbird* (Cape) was published in 1935. This had forty-four poems. Two, 'The Cuckoo' and 'The Loddon', were revisions of poems which had first appeared in *The Bird-Cage*, and seven, 'The Slow

13

Race', 'Stay, Spring', 'The Secret Wood', 'An Evening Walk', 'Sea-Wormwood', 'The River Dove', and 'The Fallen Tree' were revisions of poems from *The New Shepherd*. There were thirty-five new poems.

*Collected Poems* (Cape) appeared in 1936 and was made up of the forty-five poems from *Winter Harvest*, the forty-four from *The White Blackbird*, one poem, 'The Nest', transferred intact from *The New Shepherd*, eight revisions from the 'Wilson' books, and eight new poems. The revisions were five poems, 'The Ventriloquists', 'The Chalk-Cliff', 'August', 'Snow', 'Autumn Seeds' from *The Bird-Cage*, one poem, 'The Missel-Thrush' from *The Cuckoo Clock*, and two poems, 'The Chalk-Quarry' and 'South Downs' from *The New Shepherd*. The new poems were 'Cuckoo in May', 'Walking in Beech Leaves', 'The Echoing Cliff', 'The Elm Beetle', 'February', 'The Scarecrow', 'The Mountain', and 'Man and Cows'. There were one hundred and six poems in all.

*Nicodemus. A Mystery* (Cape) was published in 1936. Although it is not Andrew Young's only verse play, it is the only one which he wishes to survive.

*Speak to the Earth* (Cape) was published in 1939. It consisted of forty-three poems, of which thirty-seven were new, and six, revisions of poems from the 'Wilson' books; 'The Thunder Storm', 'A Wet Day', and 'The Housemartins' from *The Bird-Cage*, 'Wiltshire Downs' and 'Christmas Day' from *The Cuckoo Clock*, and 'The Gramophone' from *The New Shepherd*.

*The Green Man* (Cape), 1947, had thirty-eight poems of which seven were revisions of previously published poems. The revisions were the considerably altered 'In Moonlight' from *Thirty-One Poems*, 'The Blind Children', 'On the Hillside', 'The Day Ends' from *The Bird-Cage*, 'The Shower' from *The Cuckoo Clock*, and 'In Avebury Circle' and 'At Formby' from *The New Shepherd*. A new poem, 'The Shepherd's Hut', was a different poem from the one which had appeared with the same title in *Speak to the Earth*.

*Collected Poems* (Cape), 1950, with wood engravings by Joan Hassall, was a compilation of all the poems in *Collected Poems* (1936), *Speak to the Earth* (1939), and *The Green Man* (1947),

187 poems in all, with the play, *Nicodemus* (1936). 'The House-martins', revised for *Speak to the Earth*, was renamed 'The Swallows', 'Autumn' from *Winter Harvest* was renamed 'Penelope', 'By the Erme' was a re-writing of a much earlier poem, 'On Dartmoor', which had first appeared in *The New Shepherd*; it is very much more than a revision.

The present collection, consisting of two hundred and nine poems, and *Nicodemus*, contains the whole of *Collected Poems* (1950) and twenty-two additional poems; the poems have been arranged chronologically. The collection does not include the long poem *Into Hades* (Hart-Davis), 1952, or 'A Traveller in Time', which were published together as *Out of This World and Back* (Hart-Davis), in 1958. Of the twenty-two additional poems, seventeen have been resurrected, as they stand, from the pre-1933 books. They are 'The Leaf' from *Songs of Night*, 'On the Cliff' from *Boaz and Ruth*, 'The Bee-Orchis' and 'Daisies' from *The Death of Eli*, 'Islands', 'Cuckoo', 'Waiting', 'A Child's Voice', from *Thirty-One Poems*, 'The Tumulus' and 'Green Hellebore' from *The Bird-Cage*, 'Rother in Flood', 'At Oxford', 'On the Beaulieu Road', 'The Oak-Wood', and 'Kingley Bottom' from *The Cuckoo Clock*, and 'Round Barrows' and 'The Flint-Breaker' from *The New Shepherd*. These must all be considered as early poems, but they are not only poems in their own right, but are included in this col-lection because they are good examples of how Andrew Young's lyrical style has developed. To these are added 'In the Dingle' from Andrew Young's prose book, *A Prospect of Britain* (Hutchinson), 1956, and revisions of three poems from the early books, 'Hymn', now in the *B.B.C. Hymn Book* (1951), which appeared in its first form in *The Adversary*, 'July' from *The Bird-Cage*, and 'At Grimes Graves' from *The New Shep-herd*, which first appeared in its revised form in *A Prospect of Britain*. One poem, 'By A British Barrow in Wartime', pre-viously contributed to *The Nineteenth Century*, has never before appeared in book form.

Andrew Young has always been a great reviser. He has come back to early poems and, though generally retaining their original ideas, has often considerably altered their language.

15

There are a few striking examples of these revisions. For instance, 'The Cuckoo' first appeared in *The Bird-Cage*.

FIRST VERSION

The air was hot under the trees;
Where pale-skinned flints fell in loose screes
I stood. 'Joy, joy,' shrilled the bird-voices,
'Love, love,' hummed the air's hidden noises;
Each flower of white, sulphur and blue
Looked in my eye with 'You, you, you.'
Then first of spring and early still
'Cuckoo' called cuckoo from the hill.

This year the leaves were late and thin,
And my eye wandering softly in
Saw perched upon a topmost twig,
Small bird to have a voice so big,
The cuckoo with long tail behind,
Twig and bird aswing on the wind;
It rose and flew with outspread tail
Guiding its flight like steering sail.

I waited, listened; came again
Across the distance of the rain
That call so faint and far-away
It sounded out of yesterday;
I started with the sudden fear
Lest spring that had seemed new and near
Was gone already. Sparrow hopped
In white plum-tree and blossom dropped.

FINAL VERSION

This year the leaves were late and thin,
And my eye wandering softly in
Saw perched upon a topmost twig,
Small bird to have a voice so big,
A cuckoo with long tail behind,
Twig and bird aswing on the wind,
That rose and flew with outspread tail
Guiding his flight like steering sail.

16

I waited, listened; came again
Across the distance of the rain
'Cuckoo' so faint and far-away
It sounded out of yesterday,
Making me start with sudden fear
Lest spring that had seemed new and near,
Was gone already. A sparrow hopped
In white plum-tree and blossom dropped.

'Wiltshire Downs', a much anthologized poem, is an even more interesting example. This first appeared in its present form in *Speak to the Earth*. It is the result of merging portions of two separate poems, 'Cuckoo-Bottom' and 'Downland Shepherd', which first appeared in *The Cuckoo Clock*.

### FIRST VERSIONS
### *Cuckoo-Bottom*

The tunnelling mould-warps
Build their fresh barrows on a kicking corpse;
Where the old barrows linger
This winter sun points no long-shadowed finger.

The thudding race-horse hooves
Print on the sodden soil their lucky grooves,
But wethers chime a bell
Where Briton warriors sleep who sleep too well.

The cuckoo's double note
Loosened like bubbles from a drowning throat
Those Britons do not hear —
Cuckoos in Egypt call this time of year.

### *Downland Shepherd*

While stable-boys go thundering by
Slinging dark divots at the sky,
Like a windhover he stands still
Beside the sun, late on the hill,
And chin on hands, hands on his crook,
Tegs, shearlings, yoes cons like a book
Or sees them pass slow as a cloud,
Four hundred heads with one prayer bowed.

## *Wiltshire Downs*

The cuckoo's double note
Loosened like bubbles from a drowning throat
Floats through the air
In mockery of pipit, lark and stare.

The stable-boys thud by
Their horses slinging divots at the sky
And with bright hooves
Printing the sodden turf with lucky grooves.

As still as a windhover
A shepherd in his flapping coat leans over
His tall sheep-crook
And shearlings, tegs and yoes cons like a book.

And one tree-crowned long barrow
Stretched like a sow that has brought forth her farrow
Hides a king's bones
Lying like broken sticks among the stones.

'At Formby' shows considerable revision. There was a poem
with this title in *The New Shepherd*. It appeared again, sixteen
years later, in *The Green Man*.

How strange to walk that shore
No foot had ever trod before
Or since the sea drew back the tide;
It seemed so vast, lonely and wide
As though God were not there
To mitigate that empty sea and air.

Strange too on the coastland
Those pines no higher than my hand;
Though as I walked the trees grew taller
And I myself grew small and smaller,
Till in a high dark wood
I seemed to find again my lost childhood.

From that wide empty shore,
No foot had ever trod before
(Or since the sea drew back the tide),
I climbed the dune's soft slide
To where no higher than my hand
Wind-bitten pines grew in the clogging sand.

But farther from the beach
The trees rose up beyond my reach,
And as I walked, they still grew taller
And I myself smaller and smaller,
Till gazing up at a high wood
I felt that I had found my lost childhood.

'The Shadow' has three versions. It first appeared in *The New Shepherd* as:

### FIRST VERSION

Dark ghost,
That from tree-trunk to tree-trunk tost,
Flows with me still,
When on the shoulder of the hill
The late sunrise
Tangles its rainbows on my eyes —

A stranger,
That stalks across the hollow hanger
Crashing in silence or
Uprisen from its falling floor
To a tree-trunk will start,
So near but nearer to my heart;

Although
Your arm is like a tossing bough
When you too stand
And wave back to my waving hand,
I ask, Can you be mine,
O shade, gigantic and divine?

Then in *Winter Harvest* there was this:

Dark ghost
That from tree-trunk to tree-trunk tost,
Flows with me still,
When on the shoulder of the hill
The late sunrise
Tangles its rainbows on my eyes —

A stranger
That stalks beneath me through the hanger
Crashing in silence or
Uprisen from its falling floor
To a tree-trunk will start,
As though myself were from myself apart;

Although
Each time I wave to you below
I see you stand
And wave back with a distant hand,
I ask, Can you be mine,
O shade gigantic and divine?

The final version first came in *Collected Poems*, 1936, as follows:

FINAL VERSION

Dark ghost
That from tree-trunk to tree-trunk tost,
Flows with me still,
When on the shoulder of the hill
The late sunrise
Tangles its rainbows on my eyes —

Although
Each time I wave to you below
I see you stand
And wave back with a distant hand,
I ask, Can you be mine,
O shade gigantic and divine?

'Christmas Day' has had an interesting bibliographical history.

There is a poem in *The Cuckoo Clock* called 'Christmas Eve'
which reads

FIRST VERSION

Housed in the open shippen
   The Infant Jesus lay;
The cows stood at the hay-cribs
   Twitching the sweet hay.

First came in the shepherds
   And snow-flakes on their hair
Seemed the white angels' feathers
   That fell through the dark air.

Next came in the Magi
   And the gold crowns they wore
They took off in deep silence
   And laid upon the floor.

But as I trudged the snow-fields
   That lay in their own light,
A thorn-bush with its shadow
   Stood doubled on the night;

And I stayed on my journey
   To listen to the cheep
Of a small bird in the thorn-bush
   I woke from its puffed sleep.

This becomes 'Christmas Day' in *Speak to the Earth*.

FINAL VERSION

Last night in the open shippen
   The Infant Jesus lay,
While cows stood at the hay-crib
   Twitching the sweet hay.

As I trudged through the snow-fields
   That lay in their own light,
A thorn-bush with its shadow
   Stood doubled on the night.

And I stayed on my journey
   To listen to the cheep
Of a small bird in the thorn-bush
   I woke from its puffed sleep.

The bright stars were my angels
   And with the heavenly host
I sang praise to the Father,
   The Son and Holy Ghost.

The following poems appeared in their first versions in *Thirty-One Poems* (1922): 'In Moonlight' (as 'Full Moon') (page 187); in *The Adversary* (1923): 'Hymn'; in *The Bird-Cage* (1926): 'The Spider', 'The Wood', 'The Rain', 'The Beech', 'The Evening Star', 'The Feather', 'The Loddon', 'The Cuckoo', 'The Chalk-Cliff', 'The Ventriloquists', 'August', 'Autumn Seeds', 'Snow', 'The Swallows' (as 'The Housemartins'), 'The Thunderstorm', 'A Wet Day', 'The Blind Children', 'On the Hillside', 'The Day Ends', 'July'; in *The Cuckoo Clock* (1929): 'The Roman Wall', 'Loch Luichart', 'The Missel-Thrush', 'Wiltshire Downs', (as two poems: 'Downland Shepherd' and 'Cuckoo-Bottom'), 'Christmas Day' (as 'Christmas Eve'), 'The Shower'; in *The New Shepherd* (1931): 'Winter Morning', 'Penelope' (as 'Autumn'), 'Illic Jacet', 'The Shadow', 'The Secret Wood', 'Stay, Spring', 'The Slow Race', 'Sea Wormwood', 'An Evening Walk', 'The Fallen Tree', 'The River Dove', 'The Chalk-Quarry', 'South Downs', 'The Gramophone', 'At Formby', 'In Avebury Circle', 'At Grime's Graves'.

Ignoring the 'Wilson' books before 1926 (with the exception of the 'resurrected' poems) only twenty-two poems of *The Bird-Cage*, twenty-one of *The Cuckoo Clock*, and thirteen of *The New Shepherd* remain outside the present collection. This is small wastage for a poet who has been writing for fifty years, and is proof of remarkable consistency. Andrew Young's prolific years, at least as far as the shorter lyrics are concerned, appear to have been from 1930 to 1947.

LEONARD CLARK

The Collected Poems of
ANDREW YOUNG

## The Leaf

Sometimes an autumn leaf
  That falls upon the ground,
  Gives the heart a wound
And wakes an ancient grief.

But I weep not that all
  The leaves of autumn die,
  I only weep that I
Should live to see them fall.

## On the Cliff

Earth with my little pathway ends
    Abruptly, and I stand
Where in a wall of snow extends
    The breakage of the land.

White birds, like fragments of the cliff,
    Fly on the empty air,
Crying as though from hearts made stiff
    With straitening despair.

And far beneath me on the beach
    Sings the incessant sea,
And sighs like love that cannot reach
    To Love's eternity.

Lord, in the weakness of my words
    Let all these pray for me,
The broken cliff, the crying birds
    And the foam-mottled sea.


## The Bee-Orchis

I saw a bee, I saw a flower;
I looked again and said, For sure
Never was flower, never was bee
Locked in such immobility.

The loud bees lurched about the hill,
But this flower-buried bee was still;
I said, O Love, has love the power
To change a bee into a flower.

# Daisies

The stars are everywhere to-night,
Above, beneath me and around;
They fill the sky with powdery light
And glimmer from the night-strewn ground;
For where the folded daisies are
In every one I see a star.

And so I know that when I pass
Where no sun's shadow counts the hours
And where the sky was there is grass
And where the stars were there are flowers,
Through the long night in which I lie
Stars will be shining in my sky.

# Islands

These new songs that I sing
  Were islands in the sea
That never missed a spring,
  No, nor a century.

A starry voyager,
  I to these islands come
Knowing not by what star
  I am at last come home.

## A Child's Voice

On winter nights shepherd and I
   Down to the lambing-shed would go;
Rain round our swinging lamp did fly
   Like shining flakes of snow.

There on a nail our lamp we hung,
   And O it was beyond belief
To see those ewes lick with hot tongue
   The limp wet lambs to life.

A week gone and sun shining warm
   It was as good as gold to hear
Those new-born voices round the farm
   Cry shivering and clear.

Where was a prouder man than I
   Who knew the night those lambs were born,
Watching them leap two feet on high
   And stamp the ground in scorn?

Gone sheep and shed and lighted rain
   And blue March morning; yet to-day
A small voice crying brings again
   Those lambs leaping at play.

# Waiting

We waited for the spring,
  My love and I;
The larks were in the sky,
The lambs were on the hill:
Did we not hear them sing?
Did we not hear them cry?
Yes, yes, O yes, but still
We waited for the spring
  My love and I.

We waited for the spring,
  My love and I;
Speedwell that robs the sky,
Trumpeting daffodil
And blackthorn's blossoming,
We watched them all go by;
These came and went but still
We waited for the spring
  My wife and I.

## Cuckoo

Cuckoo, cuckoo!
Is it your double note I hear
Now far away, now near,
Now soft, now clear,
Cuckoo?

Cuckoo, cuckoo!
Laughs now through the spring's misty wood
And leaf-winged sap in flood
Your mocking mood,
Cuckoo?

Cuckoo, cuckoo!
So sits among sky-tangling trees
Our Mephistopheles
Singing at ease,
Cuckoo.

Begone, cuckoo!
For soon your bubble-note twin born,
Pricked by the June rose-thorn,
Shall burst in scorn,
Cuckoo.

## The Stars

The stars rushed forth to-night
Fast on the faltering light;
So thick those stars did lie
No room was left for sky;
And to my upturned stare
A snow-storm filled the air.

Stars lay like yellow pollen
That from a flower has fallen;
And single stars I saw
Crossing themselves in awe;
Some stars in sudden fear
Fell like a falling tear.

What is the eye of man,
This little star that can
See all those stars at once,
Multitudinous suns,
Making of them a wind
That blows across the mind?

If eye can nothing see
But what is part of me,
I ask and ask again
With a persuasive pain,
What thing, O God, am I,
This mote and mystery?

# The Last Leaf

I saw how rows of white raindrops
   From bare boughs shone,
And how the storm had stript the leaves
   Forgetting none
Save one left high on a top twig
   Swinging alone;
Then that too bursting into song
   Fled and was gone.

# Late Autumn

The boy called to his team
   And with blue-glancing share
Turned up the rape and turnip
   With yellow charlock to spare.

The long lean thistles stood
   Like beggars ragged and blind,
Half their white silken locks
   Blown away on the wind.

But I thought not once of winter
   Or summer that was past
Till I saw that slant-legged robin
   With autumn on his chest.

# The Yellow-Hammers

All up the grassy many-tracked sheep-walk,
  Low sun on my right hand, hedge on my left
  Blotted by a late leaf, else leaf-bereft,
I drove my golden flock.

Yellow-hammers, gold-headed, russet-backed,
  They fled in jerky flight before my feet,
  Or pecked in the green ranks of winter-wheat,
While I my footsteps slacked.

Myself, the road, the hedge, these flying things,
  Who led, who followed as we climbed the hill?
  Loud as their repeated trembling trill-trill
Was the swift flirt of wings.

So tame I would have touched them with my hand,
  But they were gone, darting with rise and fall;
  I followed, till at the hedge-end they all
Dispersed over the land.

There, where the hill-side scattered the sheep-walk,
  Deserted by the birds I stood to muse
  How I but now had served so sweet a use,
Driving my golden flock.

# The Flood

The winter flood is out, dully glazing the weald,
The Adur, a drowned river, lies in its bed concealed;
Fishes flowing through fences explore paddock and field.

Bushes, waist-deep in water, stand sprinkled here and there;
A solitary gate, as though hung in mid-air,
Waits idly open, leading from nowhere to nowhere.

These bushes at night-fall will have strange fish for guests,
That wagtail, tit and warbler darkened with their nests;
Where flood strays now, light-headed lapwings lifted
    crests.

But soon comes spring again; the hazel-boughs will angle
With bait of yellow catkins that in the loose winds
    dangle
And starry scarlet blossoms their blind buds bespangle;

Dogs'-mercury from the earth unfold seed-clasping fists
And green-leaved honeysuckle roll in tumbling twists
And dreams of spring shake all the seeds that sleep in
    cists.

O blue-eyed one, too well I know you will not awake,
Who waked or lay awake so often for my sake,
Nor would I ask our last leave-taking to retake.

If lesser love of flower or bird waken my song,
It is that greater love, too full to flow along,
Falls like that Adur back, flood-like, silent and strong.

# The Lane

Years and years and man's thoughtful foot,
Drip and guttering rains and mute
Shrinkage of snows, and shaggy-hoofed
Horse have sunk this lane tree-roofed
 Now patched with blossoming elder,
 Wayfaring-tree and guelder;
Lane that eases the sharp-scarped hill
Winding the slope with leisurely will.

Foot of Briton, formal Roman,
Saxon and Dane and Sussex yeoman
Have delved it deep as river-bed,
Till I walk wading to my head
 In air so close and hot
 And by the wind forgot,
It seems to me that in this place
The earth is breathing on my face.

Here I loiter a lost hour,
Listen to bird, look on a flower.
What will be left when I am gone?
A trodden root, a loosened stone
 And by the blackthorn caught
 Some gossamery thought
Of thankfulness to those dead bones
That knit hills closer than loose stones.

## The Old Tree

The wood shakes in the breeze
    Lifting its antlered heads;
Green leaf nor brown one sees
    But the rain's glassy beads.

One tree-trunk in the wood
    No tangled head uprears,
A stump of soft touchwood
    Dead to all hopes and fears.

Even the round-faced owl
    That shakes out his long hooting
With the moon cheek-a-jowl
    Could claw there no safe footing.

Riddled by worms' small shot,
    Empty of all desire,
It smoulders in its rot,
    A pillar of damp fire.

## Green Hellebore

Wind has an edge that cleaves
  Like hook of hedger, for
A blood-stain marks the leaves
  Wind-cut of hellebore.

Green with the loss of blood
  No heavy head looks up,
But in this Easter wood
  Hangs down an empty cup.


## The Tumulus

Here to the leeward of this Roman mound
  The wind is quiet
As any battle-shout that shook the ground
  Long ago nigh it.

Here the dead sleep in bones through centuries
  With earth for flesh,
Their own long woven in flower-tapestries
  And turf's green mesh.

No bugle shatters sleep for them, so surely
  They keep the peace;
I in their old decease mourn prematurely
  My own at ease.

## In Romsey Abbey

'Lady, the angel-heads
  That cusp your canopy
Are looking the other way;
  Why should not I
Stoop down and kiss your lips
  Or even your brow?
The little hound at your feet
  Would not bark Bow-wow.'

'Stranger, from the earth
  They dug me to sleep thus
In this organ-shaken church
  Like Eutychus;
Look! Time's clumsy fingers
  Broke my neck-bone;
I think that your lips too
  Would turn to stone.'

## On the Beaulieu Road

Oaks stand bearded with lichen
  Like witches that knot the birch;
But hark! the cow-bells chiming
  That call no one to church.

Oak-leaves to crown an empire
  Lie sodden as brown dulse,
While chiming bells in the distance
  Die like a fitful pulse.

## Kingley Bottom

Beneath these bine-looped yew-boughs
   Gorse blossom is outspread
Like gold that lies unguarded
   By dragons that hang dead.

All but one pterodactyl
   That hid in mist and rain
High over Kingley Bottom
   Hums like an aeroplane.


## The Oak-Wood

Tree behind tree they stand;
   Their slavish roots roll through the ground
And veined like the flat ivy's hand
   Their heavy boughs lean out around.

Is it not thus and thus
   The branched veins issuing from the heart
Like tentacles of an octopus
   Go up and down through every part?

How many saps have sunk?
   How many more shall yet run fresh
Till these trees too like this dead trunk
   Shall turn to touchwood, soft as flesh?

## Rother in Flood

Between twin banks the Rother
   With slow contentment goes;
Bush-sprinkled lakes spread this side and
     the other
   Flowing as the wind flows.

High on the upper lands
   White-cowled oasthouses stare
And piled poles in hop gardens seem like
     hands
   Whose fingers point in prayer.

Gathered by stormy weather
   The rooks and sea-gulls meet
Like black angels and white mingling
     together
   At God's last judgement-seat.


## At Oxford

Though cold December rains draw vanishing rings
   On the choked Isis that goes swirling by,
These academic gowns flap like the wings
   Of half-fledged blackbirds that attempt to fly.

# The Signpost

Snowflakes dance on the night;
   A single star
Glows with a wide blue light
   On Lochnagar.

Through snow-fields trails the Dee;
   At the wind's breath
An ermine-clad spruce-tree
   Spits snow beneath.

White-armed at the roadside
   Wails a signpost,
'To-night the world has died
   And left its ghost.'

## The Pines

The eye might fancy that those pines,
With snow-struck stems in pallid lines,
Were lit by the sunlight at noon,
Or shadow-broken gleam of the moon;
But snowflakes rustle down the air,
Circling and rising here and there
As though uncertain where to fall,
Filling the wood with a deep pall,
The wood that hastens darkness to hide all.

The hurricane of snow last night
Felled one; its roots, surprised by light,
Clutch at the air in wild embrace;
Peace like an echo fills the place
Save for the quiet labour of snow,
That falling flake on flake below
The torn limbs and the red wounds stanches,
And with a sheet the dead trunk blanches,
And lays white delicate wreaths among
     the branches.

## Loch Brandy

All day I heard the water talk
From dripping rock to rock
And water in bright snowflakes scatter
On boulders of the black Whitewater;
But louder now than these
The silent scream of the loose tumbling screes.

Grey wave on grey stone hits
And grey moth flits
Moth after moth, but oh,
What floats into that silver glow,
What golden moth
That rises with a strange majestic sloth?

O heart, why tremble with desire
As on the water shakes that bridge of fire?
The gold moth floats away, too soon
To narrow to a hard white moon
That scarce will light the path
Stumbling to where the cold mist wreathes
     the strath.

# The Star

A white mist swathed the valley;
    Each huge uncertain tree
Came looming through the darkness
    An island in a sea;
But when I climbed to Hawkley
    The stars held all the night,
Spangles and glittering ouches
    And clouds of hollow light.

I thought they were blest spirits
    Borne upward on a wind
And the white mist the cerements
    That they had left behind;
And you, your body sleeping,
    In their bright numbers moved
And with raised face I questioned,
    Which is my well-beloved.

# The Green Woodpecker

Whether that popinjay
    Screamed now at me or at his mate
I could not rightly say,
    Not knowing was it love or was it hate.

I hoped it was not love
    But hate that roused that gaudy bird;
For earth I love enough
    To crave of her at least an angry word.

## The Nest

Four blue stones in this thrush's nest
I leave, content to make the best
Of turquoise, lapis lazuli
Or for that matter of the whole blue sky.

## On the Pilgrims' Road

That I had hit the Road
    I partly knew
From a great Roman snail
    And sombre yew;
But that my steps went from
    And not towards
The shrine of good St. Thomas,
    I thought of afterwards.

So I adored to-day
    No, not his ghost,
But the saints in Westwell window,
    And her the most
Who knelt there with no head
    But was so very
Adorable a saint
    In dress of crushed strawberry.

## March Hares

I made myself as a tree,
No withered leaf twirling on me;
No, not a bird that stirred my boughs,
As looking out from wizard brows
I watched those lithe and lovely forms
That raised the leaves in storms.

I watched them leap and run,
Their bodies hollowed in the sun
To thin transparency,
That I could clearly see
The shallow colour of their blood
Joyous in love's full flood.

I was content enough,
Watching that serious game of love,
That happy hunting in the wood
Where the pursuer was the more pursued,
To stand in breathless hush
With no more life myself than tree or bush.

## Round Barrows

The prophet's cloudy hand
Was not so small
As those grave-howes that stand
Along the sky-line of the rig,
No, nor so big
Now as the shades of evening fall.

But what of their dead bones?
Not stiff and stark they lie,
But as a family,
Fathers, mothers and sons,
With indrawn knees
They lie or lean or sit at ease.


## The Flint-Breaker

After the rain was gone
The wind among the trees rained on;
I listening to that scattered tread
Heard what the old flint-breaker said
(Two years or three before):
'Some flints have water at the core.'

Did I walk that sea-bank
Where flints with fluid mouths once drank
The drop they hold apart
In rusty hollow of their heart,
And lingers too in me—
One drop of that old Nummulitic Sea?

## In Moonlight

We sat where boughs waved on the ground
But made no sound;
'They cannot shake me off,'
Shrieked the black dwarf,
Impudent elf,
That was the shadow of myself.

I said to him, 'We must go now';
But from his bough
He laughed, securely perched,
'Then you rise first;'
It seemed to me
He spoke in wicked courtesy.

We rose and 'Take my hand,' he whined,
Though like the wind
Each waving bough he leapt;
And as we stept
Down the steep track
He seemed to grow more hunched and black.

## The Spider

A single white dewdrop
That hung free on the air sang, Stop!
From twig to twig a speckled spider,
Legged like a hermit-crab, had tied her
Invisible web with WELCOME
For sign, and HOME SWEET HOME.

That spider would not stir,
Villain of her Greek theatre,
Till as I heedlessly brushed past her
She fled fast from her web's disaster
And from a twig-fork watched it swing,
Wind tangling string with string.

Now she weaves in the dark
With no light lent by a star's spark
From busy belly more than head
Geometric pattern of thin thread,
A web for wingy midge and fly,
With deadly symmetry.

# The Wood

Summer's green tide rises in flood
Foaming with elder-blossom in the wood,
And insects hawk, gold-striped and blue,
On motion-hidden wings the air looks through,
And 'Buzz, buzz, buzz',
Gaily hums Sir Pandarus,
As blue ground-ivy blossom
Bends with the weight of a bee in its bosom.

Heavy with leaves the boughs lean over
The path where midges in a loose ball hover,
And daisies and slow-footed moss
And thin grass creep across,
Till scarcely on the narrow path
The sparrow finds a dusty bath,
And caterpillars from the leaves
Arch their green backs on my coat-sleeves.

Bright as a bird the small sun flits
Through shaking leaves that tear the sky in bits;
But let the leaf-lit boughs draw closer,
I in the dark will feel no loser
With myself for companion.
Grow, leafy boughs; darken, O sun,
For here two robins mate
That winter held apart in a cold hate.

# The Rain

Fair mornings make false vows!
   When to that wood I came
I stood beneath fast-dripping boughs
   And watched the green leaves wink
   Spilling their heavy drink;
Some flowers to sleeping buds returned,
Some, lit by rain, with clear flames burned;
'Cuckoo' — again, again
   A cuckoo called his name
Behind the waving veil of dismal rain.

The rain bit yellow root
   And shone on the blue flints
And dangled like a silver fruit
   From blackened twigs and boughs;
   I watched those running rows
Splash on the sodden earth and wet
The empty snail-shells marked 'To Let',
And whitened worms that lay
   Like stalks of hyacinths,
The last end of a children's holiday.

I heard a dead man cough
   Not twenty yards away —
(A wool-wet sheep, likely enough,
   As I thought afterwards);
   But O those shrieking birds!
   And how the flowers seemed to outstare
Some hidden sun in that dim air,
As sadly the rain soaked
   To where the dead man lay
Whose cough a sudden fall of earth had
   choked.

## The Beech

Strength leaves the hand I lay on this beech-bole
   So great-girthed, old and high;
Its sprawling arms like iron serpents roll
   Between me and the sky.

One elbow on the sloping earth it leans,
   That steeply falls beneath,
As though resting a century it means
   To take a moment's breath.

Its long thin buds in glistering varnish dipt
   Are swinging up and down
While one young beech that winter left unstript
   Still wears its withered crown.

At least gust of the wind the great tree heaves
   From heavy twigs to groin;
The wind sighs as it rakes among dead leaves
   For some lost key or coin.

And my blood shivers as away it sweeps
   Rustling the leaves that cling
Too late to that young withered beech that keeps
   Its autumn in the spring.

# The Evening Star

I saw a star shine in bare trees
That stood in their dark effigies;
With voice so clear and close it sang
That like a bird it seemed to hang
Rising and falling with the wind,
Twigs on its rosy breast outlined.

An obvious moon high on the night
And haloed by a rainbow light
Sounded as loud as silver bell
And trees in flight before it fell,
Their shadows straggling on the road
Where glacier of soft moonlight flowed.

But moon nor star-untidy sky
Could catch my eye as that star's eye;
For still I looked on that same star,
That fitful, fiery Lucifer,
Watching with mind as quiet as moss
Its light nailed to a burning cross.

## The Feather

Briar, spindle and thorn tangled together
   Made dark the narrow track,
And from some hoarse-voiced rook the fallen feather
   That lay silent and black.

Gold lees left in the pink cup of dog-roses
   Nor the red campion
That the June cuckoo when his voice he loses
   Cast his white spittle on,

Nothing could lighten that track's narrow gloom,
   Except on ground or bark
Some honied light straggling through branches from
   The sun that made it dark.

# The Roman Wall

Though moss and lichen crawl
  These square-set stones still keep their serried ranks
Guarding the ancient wall,
  That whitlow-grass with lively silver pranks.

Time they could not keep back
  More than the wind that from the snow-streaked north
Taking the air for track
  Flows lightly over to the south shires forth.

Each stone might be a cist
  Where memory sleeps in dust and nothing tells
More than the silent mist
  That smokes along the heather-blackened fells.

Twitching its ears as pink
  As blushing scallops loved by Romans once
A lamb leaps to its drink
  And, as the quavering cry breaks on the stones,

Time like a leaf down-drops
  And pacing by the stars and thorn-trees' sough
A Roman sentry stops
  And hears the water lapping on Crag Lough.

# Loch Luichart

Slioch and Sgurr Mor
Hang in the air in a white chastity
Of cloud and February snow
That less to earth they seem to owe
Than to the pale blue cloud-drift or
The deep blue sky.

Though high and far they stand,
Their shadows over leagues of forest come,
Here, to a purer beauty thinned
In this true mirror, now the wind,
That held it with a shaking hand,
Droops still and dumb.

As I push from the shore
And drift (beneath that buzzard) I climb now
These silver hills for miles and miles,
Breaking hard rock to gentle smiles
With the slow motion of my prow
And dripping oar.

## Winter Morning

All is so still;
The hill a picture of a hill
With silver kine that glimmer
Now whiter and now dimmer
Through the fog's monochrome,
Painted by Cotman or Old Chrome.

Pale in the sky
The winter sun shows a round eye,
That darkens and still brightens;
And all the landscape lightens
Till on the melting meadows
The trees are seen with hard white shadows.

Though in the balk
Ice doubles every lump of chalk
And the frost creeps across
The matted leaves in silver moss,
Here where the grass is dank
The sun weeps on this brightening bank.

# Penelope

The leaves hang on the boughs
Filemot, ochreous,
Or fall and strangely greet
Green blades of winter wheat
The long buds of the beech
Point where they cannot reach.

A sad Telemachus,
I stand under the boughs;
Patient Penelope,
Her heart across the sea,
Another year unweaves
Her web of wasted leaves.

Is bud and leaf and flower
All we are waiting for?
But we shall wait again
When these are gone, and then
When they are gone and gone
Penelope alone.

## *Illic Jacet*

This was his little house;
　　Its moth-bright eye
Looks through the orchard-boughs
　　At the starry sky.

I never crossed his door
　　But still preferred
To hunt some orchid or
　　Watch for a bird.

We went one day to church
　　His friends and he;
We left him in the lurch,
　　As it seemed to me.

But still from his grave he days,
　　'You know the house;
You must one of these days
　　Drop in on us.'

## The Dead Bird

Ah, that was but the wind
Your soft down stirred,
O bird, lying with sidelong head;
These open eyes are blind,
I cannot frighten you away;
You are so very dead
I almost say
'You are not a dead *bird*.'

## The Shadow

Dark ghost
That from tree-trunk to tree-trunk tost,
Flows with me still,
When on the shoulder of the hill
The late sunrise
Tangles its rainbows on my eyes —

Although
Each time I wave to you below
I see you stand
And wave back with a distant hand,
I ask, Can you be mine,
O shade gigantic and divine?

## On White Down

In a high wood,
Wind chilling my premonitory blood,
I play at death
Closing my eyes and holding back my breath.

Ah glad surprise
To wake from death, and breathe, and open eyes
To see again
This mist-capped hill that is so bright with rain.

But from a bough
A blackbird mocks, 'Blind eyes are not enough;
You act the ghost
With sight and breathing that you never lost.'

O bird, be still;
When I would walk on an immortal hill
You drag me back
As though I had not left this dim hill-track.

## After the Funeral

Standing beneath the jewelled trees
That waved with slow mournful unease;
I lifted up my eyes to them —
The stars caught in the trees' dark stratagem.

But when I asked which is the wonder,
All stars above the earth and under
And in the vast hollow of space
Or the stern look on that defeated face;

I said, 'Not even the Milky Way
Shines like the golden streak of clay —
All, all of her that I could save —
My foot has gathered from her open grave.'

## The Sheaf

I'd often seen before
That sheaf of corn hung from the bough —
Strange in a wood a sheaf of corn
Though by the winds half torn
And thrashed by rain to empty straw.
And then to-day I saw
A small pink twitching snout
And eyes like black beads sewn in fur
Peep from a hole in doubt,
And heard on dry leaves go tat-tat
The stiff tail of the other rat.
And now as the short day grows dim
And here and there farms in the dark
Turn to a spark,
I on my stumbling way think how
With indistinguishable limb
And tight tail round each other's head
They'll make to-night one ball in bed,
Those long-tailed lovers who have come
To share the pheasants' harvest-home.

## The Burnt Leaves

They have been burning leaves,
Dead leaves the little shrew upheaves
Poking in winter for his trifling food.
And large black pools lie in the wood
As though the sky had rained down ink;
It all means nothing as I think
That more and more are left behind
To rise and rustle in the wind,
That paws them as a cat plays with a mouse,
And June will bring green leafy boughs;
Yet often as I watched them run
I thought of you, O blue-eyed one,
Or thought about my thoughts of you,
Fitful and feeble too:
For as these ran a little way and stopped
When the wind rose and dropped,
So I would think of you a little, yet
So soon forget.

# *Mist*

Rain, do not fall
Nor rob this mist at all,
That is my only cell and abbey wall.

Wind, wait to blow
And let the thick mist grow,
That fills the rose-cup with a whiter glow.

Mist, deepen still
And the low valley fill;
You hide but taller trees, a higher hill.

Still, mist, draw close;
These gain by what they lose,
The taller trees and hill, the whiter rose.

All else begone,
And leave me here alone
To tread this mist where earth and sky are one.


## *A Man with a Horse*

I wondered at the mighty horse
  So meekly since the day began
Toiling to make himself a corse,
  And then I wondered at the man.

# A Barrow on the Quantocks

Each night I pass the dead man's mound
I keep on turning round;
I almost stumble on the track
With looking back.

Although that mound of ling and stones
May hide his brittle bones,
I do not think that there he sleeps
Or wakes and peeps.

He is too intimately near
To see or touch or hear;
I only feel my blood is crossed
By his chill ghost.

It may be that all things are made
Of substance and of shade
And such a hill as I walk here
He walks elsewhere.

I know not which the substance is,
This hill of mine or his,
Nor which of us is the true ghost
In shadows lost.

## An Old Road

None ever walks this road
That used to lie open and broad
And ran along the oakshaw edge;
The road itself is now become the hedge.

Whatever brambles say
I often try to force a way,
Wading in withered leaves that spread
Over dead lovers' tracks a sighing bed.

Is it the thought of one
That I must meet when most alone
That makes me probe a place like this,
Where gossamer now gives the only kiss?

I shall see no one there
Though I had eyes to see the air,
But at the waving of a bough
Shall think I see the way she went but now.

## The Men

I sat to listen to each sound
Of leaf on twig or ground
And finch that cracked a seed
Torn from a limp and tarnished weed
And rapid flirt of wings
As bluetits flew and used as swings
The bines of old man's beard,
When suddenly I heard
Those men come crashing through the wood
And voices as they stood,
And dog that yelped and whined
At each shrill scent his nose could find;
And knowing that it meant small good
To some of us who owned that wood,
Badger, stoat, rabbit, rook and jay
And smoky dove that clattered away,
Although no ill to me at least,
I too crept off like any stealthy beast.

## Palmistry

I lifted from the ground my grass-pressed hand
And pondered, as its strange new lines I scanned,
What is foretold? What hope, what fear,
What strife, what passion is prefigured here?

## The Rat

Strange that you let me come so near
   And send no questing senses out
From eye's dull jelly, shell-pink ear,
   Fierce-whiskered snout.

But clay has hardened in these claws
   And gypsy-like I read too late
In lines scored on your naked paws
   A starry fate.

Even that snake, your tail, hangs dead,
   And as I leave you stiff and still
A death-like quietness has spread
   Across the hill.


## Killed by a Hawk

I stir them with my stick,
   These trembling feathers left behind
To show a hawk was sick,
   No more to fly except on the loose wind.

How beautiful they are
   Scattered by death yet speaking of
Quick flight and precious care
   Of those great gems, the nest-eggs, warm with love.

Feathers without a bird!
   As though the bird had flown away
From its own feathers, fired
   By strange desire for some immortal spray.

# The Forest of Dean

'Now here you could not lose your way,
Although you lost it,' seemed to say
Each path that ran to left or right
Through narrowing distance out of sight.

'Not here, not here,' whistled a thrush
And 'Never, never,' sighed a thorn-bush;
Primroses looked me in the face
With, 'O too lovely is this place.'

A larch-bough waved a loose green beard
And 'Never, never,' still I heard;
'Wayfarer, seek no more your track,
It lies each side and front and back.'

## The Farmer's Gun

The wood is full of rooks
That by their faded looks
No more on thievery will thrive,
As when they were alive,
Nor fill the air with the hoarse noise
That most of all is England's pleasant voice.

How ugly is this work of man,
Seen in the bald brain-pan,
Voracious bill,
Torn wing, uprooted quill
And host of tiny glistening flies
That lend false lustre to these empty eyes.

More delicate is nature's way
Whereby all creatures know their day,
And hearing Death call 'Come,
Here is a bone or crumb,'
Bury themselves before they die
And leave no trace of foul mortality.

## In December

I watch the dung-cart stumble by
  Leading the harvest to the fields,
That from cow-byre and stall and sty
  The farmstead in the winter yields.

Like shocks in a reaped field of rye
  The small black heaps of lively dung
Sprinkled in the grass-meadow lie
  Licking the air with smoky tongue.

This is Earth's food that man piles up
  And with his fork will thrust on her,
And Earth will lie and slowly sup
  With her moist mouth through half the year.

## The Round Barrow

A lark as small as a flint arrow
Rises and falls over this ancient barrow
And seems to mock with its light tones
The silent man of bones;

Some prince that earth drew back again
From his long strife with wind and mist and rain,
Baring for him this broad round breast
In token of her rest.

But as I think how Death sat once
And with sly fingers picked those princely bones,
I feel my bones are verily
The stark and final I.

I climbed the hill housed in warm flesh,
But now as one escaped from its false mesh
Through the wan mist I journey on,
A clanking skeleton.

72

## The Loddon

Through hoof-marked meadows that lie sodden
From winter's overflow, the Loddon
Winds by the winding pollard hedge,—
Stunt willow-trunks that line the edge,
Whose roots like buried eels are sunk,
A grove of saplings on each trunk.

Its water with a white-frothed mouth
Chewing and gnawing the uncouth
Loose sticks and straws that in disorder
Lie littered on its leaping border,
As breath of wind roughens its hide,
This way or that way makes its tide.

This way or that — But O let come
May-blossom that in buds lies dumb,
This water that laps bush and tree
Shall long have drifted to the sea;
I almost feel that I too go
Caught in its secret lapsing flow.

## The Cuckoo

This year the leaves were late and thin,
And my eye wandering softly in
Saw perched upon a topmost twig,
Small bird to have a voice so big,
A cuckoo with long tail behind,
Twig and bird aswing on the wind,
That rose and flew with outspread tail
Guiding his flight like steering sail.

I waited, listened; came again
Across the distance of the rain
'Cuckoo' so faint and far-away
It sounded out of yesterday,
Making me start with sudden fear
Lest spring that had seemed new and near
Was gone already. A sparrow hopped
In white plum-tree and blossom dropped.

## The Secret Wood

Where there is nothing more to see
Than this old earth-bound tree
That years ago dry sawdust bled
But sprouts each spring a leaf or two
As though it tried not to be dead,
Or that down-hanging broken bough
That keeps its withered leaves till now,
Like a dead man that cannot move
Or take his own clothes off,
What is it that I seek or who,
Fearing from passer-by
Intrusion of a foot or eye?
I only know
Though all men of earth's beauty speak
Beauty here I do not seek
More than I sought it on my mother's cheek.

## Stay, Spring

Stay, spring, for by this ruthless haste
You turn all good to waste;
Look, how the blackthorn now
Changes to trifling dust upon the bough.

Where blossom from the wild pear shakes
Too rare a china breaks,
And though the cuckoos shout
They will forget their name ere June is out.

That thrush, too, that with beadlike eye
Watches each passer-by,
Is warming at her breast
A brood that when they fly rob their own nest.

So late begun, so early ended!
Lest I should be offended
Take warning, spring, and stay
Or I might never turn to look your way.

# The Slow Race

I followed each detour
Of the slow meadow-winding Stour,
That looked on cloud, tree, hill,
And mostly flowed by standing still.

Fearing to go too quick
I stopped at times to throw a stick
Or see how in the copse
The last snow was the first snowdrops.

The river also tarried
So much of sky and earth it carried,
Or even changed its mind
To flow back with a flaw of wind.

And when we reached the weir
That combed the water's silver hair,
I knew I lost the race —
I could not keep so slow a pace.

## Sea Wormwood

It grew about my feet
Like frost unmelted in the summer heat;
I plucked it and such oozes
Flowed from its broken bruises
That as I turned inland
Its loosened scent was hanging from my hand.

And so I thought the people
Stayed from pea-picking by the road to Steeple,
No, not to watch the stranger
Who landed from Goldhanger,
But breathe the odorous oil
That flowing from his hand sweetened their toil.


## An Evening Walk

I never saw a lovelier sky;
The faces of the passers-by
Shine with gold light as they step west
As though by secret joy possessed,
Some rapture that is not of earth
But in that heavenly climate has its birth.

I know it is the sunlight paints
The faces of these travelling saints,
But shall I hold in cold misprision
The calm and beauty of that vision
Upturned a moment from the sorrow
That makes to-day to-day, to-morrow to-morrow.

## The Fallen Tree

The shade once swept about your boughs
Quietly obsequious
To the time-keeping sun;
Now, fallen tree, you with that shade are one.

From chalky earth as white as surf
Beneath the uptorn turf
Roots hang in empty space
Like snakes about the pale Medusa's face.

And as I perch on a forked branch,
More used to squirrel's haunch,
I think how dead you are,
More dead than upright post or fence or chair.


## To the River Dove

Swift under hollow shelf
Or spreading out to rest yourself
You flow between high ridge and ridge
To brim the heavy eyebrows of the bridge.

No, Dove, it is not mine
To stroke you with a fly and line,
A legless trunk wading your water;
I leave your fish to heron, pike and otter.

And him who haunts that inn
With 'Isaac Walton' for its sign,
Living there still as he lived once,
A wind-blown picture now, with creaking bones.

## The Stockdoves

They rose up in a twinkling cloud
And wheeled about and bowed
To settle on the trees
Perching like small clay images.

Then with a noise of sudden rain
They clattered off again
And over Ballard Down
They circled like a flying town.

Though one could sooner blast a rock
Than scatter that dense flock
That through the winter weather
Some iron rule has held together.

Yet in another month from now
Love like a spark will blow
Those birds the country over
To drop in trees, lover by lover.

## The Bird

The blackbird darted through the boughs
Trailing his whistle in a shrill dispute
'Why do you loiter near our house?'
But I was mute,
Though as he perched with sidelong head
I might have said,
'I never notice nests or lovers
In hedges or in covers;
I have enough to do
In my own way to be unnoticed too.'

## Last Snow

Although the snow still lingers
Heaped on the ivy's blunt webbed fingers
And painting tree-trunks on one side,
Here in this sunlit ride
The fresh unchristened things appear,
Leaf, spathe and stem,
With crumbs of earth clinging to them
To show the way they came
But no flower yet to tell their name,
And one green spear
Stabbing a dead leaf from below
Kills winter at a blow.

## The Knotted Ash

Is this a lover's vow?
Who else should tie it and for what,
This olive-coloured sapling in a knot,
Till now spring's sap must stoop
And bend back in a gouty loop
Rising from root to sooty-budded bough?

They may be tired of love,
Who found it not enough
To twine the glances of their eyes
Like kissing brimstone butterflies;
But death itself can not untwist
This piteous tree-contortionist.

## The Fairy Ring

Here the horse-mushrooms make a fairy ring,
　Some standing upright and some overthrown,
A small Stonehenge, where heavy black snails cling
　And bite away, like Time, the tender stone.

## The Swans

How lovely are these swans,
That float like high proud galleons
Cool in the summer heat,
And waving leaf-like feet
Divide with narrow breasts of snow
In a smooth surge
This water that is mostly sky;
So lovely that I know
Death cannot kill such birds,
It could but wound them, mortally.

## Eryngo

I came on that blue-headed plant
   That lovers ate to waken love,
Eryngo; but I felt no want,
   A lovesick swain, to eat thereof.

## Young Oats

These oats in autumn sown,
That stood through all the winter's dearth
In so small ranks of green
That flints like pigmies' bones lay bare
And greater stones were seen
To change to hares and rise and run,
To-day to such a height are grown
That drawn up by the sun,
That Indian conjuror,
The field is levitated from the earth.

## The Stones

Though the thick glacier,
That filled the mountain's rocky jaws
And lifted these great rocks like straws
And dropped them here,
Has shrunk to this small ale-brown burn,
Where trout like shadows dart and turn,
The stones in awkward stance
Still wait some starry circumstance
To bring the ice once more
And bear them to a distant shore.

## *The Copse*

Here in the Horseshoe Copse
The may in such a snow-storm drops
That every stick and stone
Becomes a tree with blossom of its own.


And though loose sun-spots sway
The night so lasts through all the day
That no bird great or small
Sings in these trees but is a nightingale.

Time might be anything,
Morning or night, winter or spring;
One who in this copse strays
Must walk through many months of night and days.

## The Paps of Jura

Before I crossed the sound
I saw how from the sea
These breasts rise soft and round,
Not two but three;

Now, climbing, I clasp rocks
Storm-shattered and sharp-edged,
Grey ptarmigan their flocks,
With starved moss wedged;

And mist like hair hangs over
One barren breast and me,
Who climb, a desperate lover,
With hand and knee.


## The Track

Trodden by man and horse
Tracks change their course
As rivers change their bed;
And this that I now tread,
Where the lean roots obtrude,
Was not the first track through the wood.

There older traces flow,
Where ghosts may go
But no one else save I;
And as in turn I try
Each faint and fainter track,
Through what long ages I fall back.

## The Sunbeams

The tired road climbed the hill
Through trees with light-spots never still,
Gold mouths that drew apart and singled
And ran again and met and mingled,
Two, three or five or seven,
No other way than souls that love in heaven.

Sunny and swift and cool
They danced there like Bethesda's pool;
Ah, if in those pale kissing suns
My halting feet could bathe but once
No slender stick would crack,
My footstep falling on its brittle back.

## The Dark Wood

O wood, now you are dark with summer
Your birds grow dumber
And ink-stained leaves of sycamore
Slide slowly down and hit your floor;
But there are other signs I mark,
In ivy with sunlight wet
And dried rains streaming down your bark,
A withered limb, a broken shoulder,
Signs that since first we met
Even you, O wood, have grown a little older.

## The White Blackbird

Gulls that in meadows stand,
The sea their native land,
Are not so white as you
Flitting from bough to bough,
You who are white as sin
To your black kith and kin.

## Wood and Hill

Nowhere is one alone
And in the closest covert least,
But to small eye of bird or beast
He will be known;
To-day it was for me
A squirrel that embraced a tree
Turning a small head round;
A hare too that ran up the hill,
To his short forelegs level ground,
And with tall ears stood still.
But it was birds I could not see
And larks that tried to stand on air
That made of wood and hill a market-square.


## Mole-Hills on the Downs

Here earth in her abundance spills
Hills on her hills,
Till every hill is overgrown
With small hills of its own;
Some old with moss and scorpion-grass,
Some new and bare and brown,
And one where I can watch the earth
Like a volcano at its birth
Still rise by falling down;
And as by these small hills I pass
And take them in my stride
I swell with pride,
Till the great hills to which I lift my eyes
Restore my size.

## Thistledown

Silver against blue sky
These ghosts of day float by,
Fitful, irregular,
Each one a silk-haired star,
Till from the wind's aid freed
They settle on their seed.

Not by the famished light
Of a moon-ridden night
But by clear sunny hours
Gaily these ghosts of flowers
With rise and swirl and fall
Dance to their burial.

# The Tree

Tree, lend me this root,
That I may sit here at your foot
And watch these hawking flies that wheel
And perch on the air's hand
And red-thighed bees
That fan the dust with their wings' breeze.
Do you not feel me on your heel,
My bone against your bone?
Or are you in such slumber sunk,
Woodpeckers knocking at your trunk
Find you are not at home?
To winds you are not dumb;
Then tell me, if you understand:
When your thick timber has been hewn,
Its boards in floors and fences sewn,
And you no more a tree,
Where will your dryad be?

## Fenland

Where sky is all around
And creeps in dykes along the ground,
I see trees stand outlined
Too distant to be tossed with wind.

And farther still than these
Stand but the tops of other trees,
As on the ocean's rim
Vessels half-sunk in water swim.

Where there is so much sky
And earth so level to my eye,
Trees and trees farther hide
Far down the steep world's mountain-side.

## The Dead Crab

A rosy shield upon its back,
That not the hardest storm could crack,
From whose sharp edge projected out
Black pin-point eyes staring about;
Beneath, the well-knit cote-armure
That gave to its weak belly power;
The clustered legs with plated joints
That ended in stiletto points;
The claws like mouths it held outside:
I cannot think this creature died
By storm or fish or sea-fowl harmed
Walking the sea so heavily armed;
Or does it make for death to be
Oneself a living armoury?

## In Teesdale

No, not to-night,
Not by this fading light,
Not by those high fells where the forces
Fall from the mist like the white tails of horses.

From that dark slack
Where peat-hags gape too black
I turn to where the lighted farm
Holds out through the open door a golden arm.

No, not to-night,
To-morrow by daylight;
To-night I fear the fabulous horses
Whose white tails flash down the steep water-courses.

## A Windy Day

This wind brings all dead things to life,
Branches that lash the air like whips
And dead leaves rolling in a hurry
Or peering in a rabbits' bury
Or trying to push down a tree;
Gates that fly open to the wind
And close again behind,
And fields that are a flowing sea
And make the cattle look like ships;

Straws glistening and stiff
Lying on air as on a shelf
And pond that leaps to leave itself;
And feathers too that rise and float,
Each feather changed into a bird,
And line-hung sheets that crack and strain;
Even the sun-greened coat,
That through so many winds has served,
The scarecrow struggles to put on again.

## The Ruined Chapel

From meadows with the sheep so shorn
They, not their lambs, seem newly born
Through the graveyard I pass,
Where only blue plume-thistle waves
And headstones lie so deep in grass
They follow dead men to their graves,
And as I enter by no door
This chapel where the slow moss crawls
I wonder that so small a floor
Can have the sky for roof, mountains for walls.

## The Comet

Why do I idly stand
And digging with my finger-tips
Tear the tree-trunk in strips?
Because such touchwood soft and damp
I once would stuff in a clay lamp
And blow on it with fiery face
To coax a sparkling light
And through the darkness race,
That lit lamp in my hand
A comet streaming through the autumn night.

## Gossip

The wind shaking the gate
Impatiently as though in haste and late
Shook and shook it making it rattle,
And all the other tittle-tattle
It rushed to tell, —
Of how mahogany chestnuts fell
And how the gamekeeper
Had crackling paper here and there and there
To frighten pheasants back into the wood,
And how the flapping scarecrow stood
And guarding seeds from harm
Saluted with a broken arm,
And how the thin-voiced lamb
Still in the autumn sucked his dam,
A late and casual love-begot,
All that I heard and proudly thought
That I, a man, whom most things hate,
Shared country gossip with the wind and gate.

# By the Tyne

What foolish birds were they
That build these nests exposed to day,
A score on every tree
So darkly clear between the river and me?

Not birds that haunt these woods,
But heavy, hurrying winter floods
With their foam-hissing billows
Left these wild driftwood nests on the lean willows.

# Ploughing in Mist

Pulling the shoulder-sack
Closer about his neck and back,
He called out to his team
That stamped off dragging the weigh-beam;
And as he gripped the stilts and steered
They plunged in mist and disappeared,
Fading so fast away
They seemed on a long journey gone,
Not to return that day;
But while I waited on
The jingle of loose links I caught,
And suddenly on the hill-rise,
Pale phantoms of the mist at first,
Man and his horses burst
As though before my eyes
Creation had been wrought.

## The Eagle

He hangs between his wings outspread
   Level and still
And bends a narrow golden head,
   Scanning the ground to kill.

Yet as he sails and smoothly swings
   Round the hill-side,
He looks as though from his own wings
   He hung down crucified.

## The Fear

How often I turn round
To face the beast that bound by bound
Leaps on me from behind,
Only to see a bough that heaves
With sudden gust of wind
Or blackbird raking withered leaves.

A dog may find me out
Or badger toss a white-lined snout;
And one day as I softly trod
Looking for nothing stranger than
A fox or stoat I met a man
And even that seemed not too odd.

And yet in any place I go
I watch and listen as all creatures do
For what I cannot see or hear,
For something warns me everywhere
That even in my land of birth
I trespass on the earth.


## On Middleton Edge

If this life-saving rock should fail
Yielding too much to my embrace
And rock and I to death should race,
The rock would stay there in the dale
While I, breaking my fall,
Would still go on
Farther than any wandering star has gone.

## A Heap of Faggots

Faggots of ash, elm, oak
That dark loose snowflakes touch and soak,
An unlit fire they lie
With cold inhospitality.

Nothing will light them now,
Sticks that with only lichen glow
And crumble to touchwood
Soft and unfit for fire's food.

And with wren, finch and tit
And all the silent birds that sit
In this snow-travelled wood
I warm myself at my own blood.

## Black Rock of Kiltearn

They named it Aultgraat — Ugly Burn,
This water through the crevice hurled
Scouring the entrails of the world —
Not ugly in the rising smoke
That clothes it with a rainbowed cloak.
But slip a foot on frost-spiked stone
Above this rock-lipped Phlegethon
And you shall have
The Black Rock of Kiltearn
For tombstone, grave
And trumpet of your resurrection.

## In the Fallow Field

I went down on my hands and knees
Looking for trees,
Twin leaves that, sprung from seeds,
Were now too big
For stems much thinner than a twig.
These soon with chamomile and clover
And other fallow weeds
Would be turned over;
And I was thinking how
It was a pity someone should not know
That a great forest fell before the plough.


## Autumn

A new Teiresias and unreproved,
Not stricken by the goddess that I loved,
To-day I looked and saw the earth undress
With intimate and godlike carelessness.

# NICODEMUS
## A Mystery

JOHN as an old man

JOHN as a young man

NICODEMUS

A BLIND MAN

SIMON PETER

JUDAS

CAIAPHAS, the High Priest

ANNAS, formerly the High Priest

Clerk and Members of the Sanhedrin

Constables

SAUL

An Angel

*In a house. Darkness; then a spot of light discloses* JOHN, *as an old man, writing his Gospel; he sits at the side.*

JOHN Now when he was in Jerusalem at the passover, in the feast day, many believed in his name, when they saw the miracles which he did. But Jesus did not commit himself unto them, because he knew all men, and needed not that any should testify of man: for he knew what was in man. There was a man of the Pharisees, named Nicodemus, a ruler of the Jews; the same came to Jesus by night and said unto him —

What did he say? —
Where are the notes that Peter sent from Rome?
— He too was crucified — . I see
He writes a sprawling hand like Paul. — 'Rabbi,
We know thou art a teacher come from God.'
And what did Jesus say? 'Except a man
Be born again — '; that puzzled Nicodemus.
'How can a man be born when he is old?'
I was not born till I was nearly thirty;
Poor Nicodemus had a lot to learn.
Then Jesus spoke about the wind. 'The wind — '
He said, 'it bloweth where it listeth — '
That was a night of wind; I thought the wind
Would blow the Paschal moon out of the sky;
Trees kept their backs to it, bending like divers.
But we were snug indoors; we felt it strange,
We fishermen, to be there in the city,
Not in the wave-lit darkness of the lake.
It was the night that Simon cooked the supper;
He raised the cover from a dish of eels;
'See, they have lost their heads like John the Baptist,'

Said Andrew; and we all looked grave at first,
Till Jesus smiled, and then we burst out laughing.
Fishers of men!
We little thought of the rich lustrous fish
That even then was nosing at the net.
Supper was ended and we sang our hymn;
The hymn we often sang;
We were a happy band of brothers then;
> 'Behold how good a thing it is,
> and how becoming well' —
No sooner had we sung it than a knock
Came at the door. 'Go, John,' the Master said,
'We have a visitor; see who he is.'

SCENE I

*Outside the door of a house. It is a windy night with a full moon.
A hymn is being sung in the house.*

(NICODEMUS *enters during the singing*)

> Behold how good a thing it is,
> and how becoming well,
> Together such as brethren are
> in unity to dwell!

> Like precious ointment on the head,
> that down the beard did flow,
> Ev'n Aaron's beard, and to the skirts
> did of his garments go.

> As Hermon's dew, the dew that doth
> on Sion's hills descend;
> For there the blessing God commands,
> life that shall never end.

(NICODEMUS *enters hesitatingly, knocks at the door, and*
JOHN, *as a young man, opens it*)

NICODEMUS Is this where Jesus lodges?
JOHN Nicodemus!
NICODEMUS Hush, do not shout my name. I see you know me.
JOHN Know you? Surely I know you; only —
NICODEMUS You are surprised to see me. Have I not
Seen you with Jesus? You are His disciple?
What is your name?
JOHN John
NICODEMUS A relative of John the Baptist?
JOHN A distant cousin.
NICODEMUS Indeed? John was a most outspoken man,
And he is dead. It does not always do
To say too much. Is Jesus in the house?
JOHN You think He says too much?
NICODEMUS He might say less; and yet I do not know.
JOHN Is He in danger? Is that why you come?
NICODEMUS No, not immediately; but who can tell?
JOHN You come to warn Him?
NICODEMUS Listen! what is that sound?
JOHN Only the wind.
NICODEMUS No, no; that other sound; that tap-tap-tapping.
JOHN I hear it; somewhere down the street.
NICODEMUS Now it has stopped; no, it begins again.
JOHN It sounds like someone knocking.
NICODEMUS There, someone has passed that lighted window.
JOHN It is his stick that taps.
NICODEMUS He stops; he peers about him like a bird.
Stand in the shadow till he passes.
JOHN No need; the man is blind.

( *The* BLIND MAN *enters*)

BLIND MAN Who says that I am blind? If I am blind,
I see you well enough, you standing there.
I raise my stick; ah, does that frighten you?
You will not speak lest I should beg for money;
I do not beg at night when I am rich.

Listen; these coins chink sweeter than house-sparrows,
They sing like nightingales.
Will you not speak?
God curse this world; I say God curse this world
Where blind men make the others deaf and dumb.
I see you there; you think that I am blind;
I am not blind except I cannot see.
God gave me eyes; I feel them with my finger;
They died the day that I was born. Alas,
That you should stand and feel me with your eyes
And my eyes should be dumb and cannot answer.
I know the dogs better than I know men;
We share the street and have our meals together;
They do not even know that I am blind.
I know you stand there, for you stand so still.
A curse upon you, you that I heard speak
And you that have been silent like a spirit.
But I know someone who will speak to me,
And one day I shall meet him — Jesus the Prophet
Have you not heard He gives sight to the blind?
He is not such as you who grudge us sight.
You mock at me because you think me blind;
My eyes are only blind until I see Him.

(*The* BLIND MAN *goes out*)

JOHN What shall I do? Shall I go after him?
NICODEMUS No, let him go; I know the fellow well;
He sits all day at the Gate Beautiful;
His blindness is a profitable business.
Your Master has more sense than heal him — Yet,
Why not, why not? Quick, call him back.
JOHN You want him back?
NICODEMUS I want to see a miracle.
JOHN Blind man, blind man! — I cannot hear his stick.
Blind man, blind man! — can he have gone so far?
NICODEMUS The man is sly; he listens like a mouse.
JOHN Blind man, blind man, if you would have your sight —
It is the wind that blows my voice away.

Blind man! Hello! Jesus is here.

NICODEMUS  Hush, you will wake the street. The man is gone;
Perhaps he will come back. In any case —

(SIMON PETER *comes out from the house*)

SIMON PETER  Who calls on Jesus?

JOHN  Simon!

SIMON PETER  John, was it you? I thought it was your voice.

JOHN  I called to a blind man who passed just now.

SIMON PETER  What did he want?

JOHN  Simon, go in; I will explain.

SIMON PETER  Who have you there? Someone stands in the
shadow.

JOHN  Go in just now; we have a wonderful guest.

SIMON PETER  What guest? Who is he?

JOHN  Someone whose name you know: it is — —

NICODEMUS  Tell him to close the door.

SIMON PETER  The wonderful guest tells me to close the door.
But hurry, John; your supper will get cold.

(SIMON PETER *goes into the house, closing the door*)

NICODEMUS  Who is that man?

JOHN  His name is Simon; Jesus calls him Peter.

NICODEMUS  Peter; that means a rock.

JOHN  I know; He says that on this rock —

NICODEMUS  What rock? You mean that man?

JOHN  I know that it sounds strange; He said —
But no; you would not understand. Come in.
Jesus would like to speak to you.

NICODEMUS  He is at supper; I will come again.

JOHN  Will you not join us?

NICODEMUS  I have already supped.

JOHN  Not even in a cheerful cup? I know
That Jesus will be disappointed.

NICODEMUS  Tell me one thing; why do you follow Jesus?

JOHN  It was because of John the Baptist first.

NICODEMUS  But why because of him?

JOHN  One day, when we were standing by the Jordan,
John and my cousin Andrew and myself,

109

We saw a man pass by, tall as a spirit;
He did not see us though he passed quite near;
Indeed we thought it strange;
His eyes were open but he looked on nothing;
And as he passed, John, pointing with his finger,
Cried — I can hear him cry it now —
'Behold, The Lamb of God!'
NICODEMUS And He, what did He say? What did He do?
JOHN Nothing; we watched Him slowly climb the hill;
His shadow fell before Him; it was evening.
Sometimes He stopped
To raise His head to the home-flying rooks
Or greet a countryman with plough on shoulder.
NICODEMUS John said, 'Behold, the Lamb of God'?
JOHN He said so.
NICODEMUS And from that day you followed Him?
JOHN No, that was afterwards in Galilee.
NICODEMUS But tell me why; why did you follow Him?
JOHN I think it was our feet that followed Him;
It was our feet; our hearts were too afraid.
Perhaps indeed it was not in our choice;
He tells us that we have not chosen Him,
But He has chosen us. I only know
That as we followed Him that day He called us
We were not walking on the earth at all;
It was another world,
Where everything was new and strange and shining;
We pitied men and women at their business,
For they knew nothing of what we knew —
NICODEMUS Perhaps it was some miracle He did.
JOHN It was indeed; more miracles than one;
I was not blind and yet He gave me sight;
I was not deaf and yet He gave me hearing;
Nor was I dead, yet me He raised to life.

(JUDAS *enters from the house and looks about suspiciously,
opening and closing the door carefully. He looks about him
and goes out*)

110

NICODEMUS  Who is that man?
JOHN  Judas Iscariot.
NICODEMUS  Is he one of your company?
JOHN  He is.
NICODEMUS  Why did he look like that? Where is he going?
JOHN  I do not know. He often walks at night.
NICODEMUS  If he has left the house, supper is ended.
JOHN  Listen; they sing the hymn.

(*A hymn is sung from the house*)

> The Lord's my shepherd, I'll not want,
>     He makes me down to lie
> In pastures green; he leadeth me
>     the quiet waters by.
>
> My soul he doth restore again;
>     and me to walk doth make
> Within the paths of righteousness,
>     ev'n for his own name's sake.
>
> Yea, though I walk in death's dark vale,
>     yet will I fear none ill;
> For thou art with me; and thy rod
>     and staff me comfort still.
>
> My table thou hast furnishèd
>     in presence of my foes;
> My head thou dost with oil anoint,
>     and my cup overflows.
>
> Goodness and mercy all my life
>     shall surely follow me:
> And in God's house for evermore
>     my dwelling-place shall be.

JOHN  Nicodemus!
NICODEMUS  Nothing, nothing; the music wrought on me.
I shiver too in the night wind;

And that man who went out, he bodes some evil.
The night is growing late; it is too late;
To-morrow I will come —
JOHN To-morrow He returns to Galilee.
NICODEMUS But He will come again.
JOHN But not this hour. O Nicodemus, look!
A miracle; you asked a miracle;
Look, look, the wind has blown the door wide open.
NICODEMUS A miracle?
JOHN He used the wind to work a miracle;
Even the wind obeys Him.
NICODEMUS I scarcely think it is a miracle.
JOHN It is, it is.

(SIMON PETER *appears at the open door*)

SIMON PETER John, John, will you stop railing in the street?
There is no miracle about the door.
I opened it myself. The wind's hand too
Plucked at it; we both opened it at once.
I told the Master of our visitor;
Why do you keep him standing at the door?
What is that sound?
JOHN The blind man coming back; you hear his stick
Tap-tapping; he is coming down the street;
Now it has stopped.
I will stay here and speak to him. You, Peter,
Take Nicodemus in, if he will go.
SIMON PETER Nicodemus!
NICODEMUS I — I will go in.

(PETER *and* NICODEMUS *go into the house;* JOHN *waits till
the* BLIND MAN *enters*)

JOHN Blind man.
BLIND MAN Ah, voice, we meet again. Still standing there?
Have you no feet to walk about?
Good voice, take care of your invisible throat;
Voices can catch a cold and cough and spit.
Voice, be a voice and speak. Where are you?

I cannot see to hit you with my stick.

JOHN Keep your stick quiet.

BLIND MAN A stick? a serpent; this is Moses' serpent;
Jump quick or he will bite your heels.

JOHN Listen. I heard you ask —

BLIND MAN And why did you not answer? Tell me that.
And where is your voice's friend, the other voice,
The dumb voice that cannot speak? Is he about?
Hiss at him, serpent.

JOHN Keep your stick quiet and listen.

BLIND MAN Listen? What does a blind man do but listen?
I listen like an echo in a cave;
I am a drum that listens to be struck.
And when did you, you paste-faced hypocrite,
Listen to me? Have you not seen me sit
Outside the Temple, mewing like a cat,
'An alms, an alms, for God's sake give an alms;
Pity a poor blind beggar.' And did you listen?

JOHN I might say something for your good.

BLIND MAN All day I sit there with my sleeping eyes
And look up at the sun. God thinks I pray.
But when night comes
And I can rattle money in my purse,
Ah, then I am a king, night is my kingdom.
O I can see to spy a tavern door,
And there I meet my friends; I know their voices;
Some blind like me, some deaf or dumb or halt;
One has a palsy, he trembles like an earthquake;
And there is one that often drops down dead;
And there we sing our — well, not our psalms.

JOHN I do not doubt it, friend.

BLIND MAN You cannot see by night, but I can see;
O that my eyes could see that Man called Jesus.

JOHN Perhaps they will; I think they will;
But not to-night.

BLIND MAN No, not to-night; I will be healed by day;
I should be only half-healed in the dark.
My eyes must look up at the blessed sun.

They say it is no bigger than an apple
And made of fire. How can a fire be round?
I do not understand about the moon;
How can men see the moon when it is night?
No, it must be by day my eyes are born.
How they will sit on either side my head,
Those new-born twins, and look up at the sun!
But with two eyes will I not see two suns?
JOHN Both the same sun.
BLIND MAN But, God forbid, what if one brat should die,
Should I see half the sun?
JOHN You will see all the sun.
BLIND MAN For I have heard men say that they saw only
Half of the moon.
JOHN No, with one eye you would see all the sun.
BLIND MAN Well, God is wise, giving the blind two eyes.
I must see Jesus.
JOHN If you see Jesus, you will see indeed.
Good-night, my friend.

(*The* BLIND MAN *goes out;* NICODEMUS *comes from the house*)

JOHN Nicodemus!
NICODEMUS My name! Who speaks the name I had forgotten?
My eyes are stupid coming from the light.
John, is it you? Have you been waiting here:
Still waiting? O how long ago it is
Since you and I stood talking at this door.
It was another life. I did not know
Your Master then; O John, I know Him now.
I had a mother once and she is dead;
I think she did not bear me till this hour.
Or 'born again' was what the Master said;
Have I been born again? O God, I pray
I be not cast out like a stillborn child.
He is to blame to let me go — But no;
I cannot now go back: never again.
It was a stillborn child my mother bore,
But I am come alive to-night. O John,

Not only I am born again to-night,
The world is born again. Look at the stars;
Though small they jostle in the sky for room,
Shining so bright, they drop down through the air;
Are they not born again? Look at the street;
The stones are nestling down to their hard sleep,
Stone nudging neighbour stone, whispering 'Friend,
Are we not born to-night?' Look at the door,
An open sepulchre; I went in dead,
Now I come out again and walk in heaven.
Who could have thought that our poor earth was heaven?
I kiss you, John, my brother.

(JUDAS *enters,* *looks at* NICODEMUS *and slowly passes into the house*)

NICODEMUS Who was that man?
JOHN Judas;
I told you that he often walks by night.
NICODEMUS Can corpses walk in heaven?
JOHN What do you mean?
It was the moonlight on his face.
NICODEMUS I fear that man.
JOHN Why do you fear him? He is one of us.
NICODEMUS Of us? he too? Has he been born again?
JOHN Why do you ask of him?
NICODEMUS I do not know;
I cannot tell you more than that I ask;
Or is it that I ask about myself?
No, no; go, brother John, back to the Master
And tell Him that I walk to-night in heaven.

(NICODEMUS *goes out;* JOHN, *looking after him, enters the house, and closes the door*)

*As in Prelude I*

JOHN (*writing*) Then they sought to take him: but no man laid hands on him, because his hour was not yet come. And many of the people believed on him, and said, When Christ cometh, will he do more miracles than these which this man hath done? The Pharisees heard that the people murmured such things concerning him: and the Pharisees and chief priests sent officers to take him.

How clearly I remember; I was there
Outside the door, where Nicodemus told me;
He said that he might call me as a witness;
He did not call me.
I saw the constables go out to take Him;
'Make way, make way,' they cried, pushing a path,
Until the people closing in like water
Hid them from sight; I saw them come again;
They shuffled in with slow uncertain steps,
But Jesus was not with them. —
How costly is this parchment that I write on;
I must write nothing but the words He spoke,
Lest men living in far-off lands and ages
Should read this Gospel I am writing now
And blame my wasted words. —
I think it was the third day of the Feast;
I never saw so great a throng before.
I heard the Levites blow the silver trumpets,
And all the people waving myrtle branches,
That stirred the sleepy dust about their feet,
Flowed on toward the golden Candelabra
Singing the harvest hymn. When that was ended,
Nicodemus came and gripped me by the arm;
We looked more than we spoke.
And then the Council entered; Caiaphas,
As High Priest for that year; then Annas followed,
His white beard streaming like a waterfall,

Then Summas, Alexander, Datan
And others that I could not name.
They took their seats. Then Caiaphas arose,
Lifting his hand, and all stood up to pray.

*The Hall of Hewn Stones*

> (JOHN *stands at the door, which opens to the Temple court.
> Outside people pass, waving branches and singing a hymn*)

Thou crownest the year with thy goodness: and thy clouds
drop fatness.

They shall drop upon the dwellings of the wilderness: and
the little hills shall rejoice on every side.

The folds shall be full of sheep: the valleys also shall stand so
thick with corn, that they shall laugh and sing.

> (NICODEMUS *enters*)

NICODEMUS John.
JOHN Nicodemus.
NICODEMUS What does the Master say?
JOHN His hour is not yet come.
NICODEMUS You are prepared to be a witness?
JOHN I am. But, Nicodemus —
NICODEMUS But what?
JOHN Remember when you came to Him that night.
NICODEMUS Remember! How can I forget that night?
I live there yet;
No sun for me has risen on that night;
It is still night; that night.
JOHN Then be yourself the witness; why not now
Come out into the light as His disciple?
NICODEMUS I will, but — is the time now ripe?
He says His hour is not yet come.
Here in the Council I am a listening ear;
I can report. And meantime I can work

In other ways. Joseph of Arimathea,
Last night I sounded him — But see, they come,
Caiaphas, Annas and the rest.

(CAIAPHAS, ANNAS, *the* CLERK *and other members of the
Sanhedrin enter*)

CAIAPHAS Why, here is Nicodemus.
NICODEMUS The High Priest's servant; and, Annas, yours.
ANNAS Mine too? As Master of the Waterworks
Take care there is no poison in the water.

(*All take their seats.* CONSTABLES *stand near the door*)

CAIAPHAS Rise, let us pray.
True is it that Thou art the Lord our God and the God of our
Fathers: our King and the King of our fathers: our Redeemer
and the Redeemer of our fathers: our Maker and the Rock of our
salvation. A new song did they that were redeemed sing to Thy
name by the sea shore. For the sake of our fathers who trusted
in Thee, and Thou taughtest them the statutes of life, Have
mercy upon us and enlighten our darkness. Blessed be the Lord,
who in love chose His people Israel. Amen.
ALL Amen.
CAIAPHAS Apologies for absence.
CLERK Gamaliel writes to say he has a cold,
And Joseph of Arimathea writes to say
He has a chill; both beg to be excused.
NICODEMUS Why are these brethren absent from our Coun-
cil?
CAIAPHAS One has a cold, the other has a chill.
NICODEMUS I fear they do not favour these proceedings.
ANNAS No more do you; yet you are here.
CAIAPHAS The Clerk will read the minutes of last meeting.
CLERK On the eleventh day of Tishri, in the Hall of Hewn
Stones; at which time and place the Sanhedrin met and was duly
constituted by prayer; the High Priest presided, and there were
also present Annas, Nicodemus, Summas, Alexander, Datan,
Gamaliel, Joseph of Arimathea, Nepthalim, Cyris and other
members. The High Priest reported that on the Day of Atone-

ment He had entered the Holy of Holies. Estimates for repairing the pipes that drain the High Altar were submitted; these were referred to the Finance Committee. Following a report sent from the Sanhedrin of Capernaum and the hearing of witnesses a discussion arose about a man called Jesus, said to be an agitator of the people. Nicodemus moved that the report be left on the table; this was not seconded. Annas then moved that as Jesus might be present at the forthcoming Feast of Tabernacles the matter be brought up at the next meeting. This was seconded and carried. There being no other business the Sanhedrin adjourned to meet on the eighteenth of Tishri in the Hall of Hewn Stones at the hour of Evening Sacrifice. The meeting closed with prayer.

CAIAPHAS  Is it your pleasure that I sign these minutes?
ALL  Agreed, agreed.
CAIAPHAS  The only business rising from these minutes
Is the report concerning this man, Jesus.
Since the last meeting of the Sanhedrin
I took it on myself,
Seeing the charges made in the report
Were of so serious a character,
To have it copied out and circulated
Among the members; it is in your hands.
NICODEMUS  Has this Man come up to the Feast?
CAIAPHAS  I hear He came two days ago.
NICODEMUS  And yet I see the charge against Him here,
That He observes no Sabbath-days or Feasts;
How can that be if He comes to the Feast?
ANNAS  He is a most notorious Sabbath-breaker.
CAIAPHAS  That matter was discussed at the last meeting.
Fathers and brethren,
I take it you have studied the report;
Are you prepared to come to a decision?
ALL  Agreed, agreed.
ANNAS  Then, Caiaphas, I rise to make a motion.
I need not now take up the Council's time
Traversing what I said at our last meeting;
My views were clearly voiced on that occasion;

So at this juncture I will merely move
This Jesus be sent for and brought before us.
NICODEMUS I, Caiaphas, would second that. But first,
Before you put the motion to the meeting,
I have a witness.
CAIAPHAS Another witness? We have heard enough.
NICODEMUS Those witnesses were on one side.
ANNAS The right side.
NICODEMUS That does not yet appear.
ANNAS It shall.
CAIAPHAS Order! I call you both to order. Fathers,
Is it your will to hear a further witness?
NICODEMUS I claim the right; can you deny my right?
ANNAS Or mine?
CAIAPHAS You too? You too would call a witness?
ANNAS Why not, if Nicodemus claims the right?
CAIAPHAS We will hear both. You, Annas, call your witness.
ANNAS Fathers, at the last meeting of our Council
We heard such evidence of this blasphemer
It burnt our ears; it might have singed our beards;
Who would have thought we needed to hear more?
But Nicodemus says 'All on one side,'
As though white were not white and black not black.
That he would call — mark the effrontery! —
One of this Man's disciples as a witness,
A lying tongue in our holy convocation,
An angel whispered in my ear.
NICODEMUS An angel? A spy, a snake;
Behold a High Priest changed to a snake-charmer!
He keeps a garden full of snakes.
ANNAS You, Nicodemus, hide behind your wealth,
But God will call you one day to account.
CAIAPHAS Order! Proceed.
ANNAS And so I am prepared.
I have a witness; fathers, take note of him,
A young man with a future, Saul of Tarsus.

(SAUL *enters*)

120

CAIAPHAS  Your name is Saul? you come from Tarsus?
SAUL  Saul is my name; I come from Tarsus.
NICODEMUS  Why is he blinking like an owl?
ANNAS  He is half-blind with studying our Law.
CAIAPHAS  What is your occupation?
SAUL  A student.
CAIAPHAS  Who is your professor?
SAUL  Gamaliel.
CAIAPHAS  Gamaliel is not here to vouch for you.
ANNAS  He has a cold, a most convenient cold;
But I can vouch for him.
CAIAPHAS  You know the Man called Jesus.
SAUL  I know Him; I am His disciple.
CAIAPHAS  What!
SAUL  None follows Him more faithfully than I.
CAIAPHAS  What are you saying? Are you mad?
Here, Annas, is a change of wind.
SAUL  No, Caiaphas, I am not mad.
I follow Him about like His own shadow;
I drink His words as a dog drinks water;
They change to gall and wormwood in my belly.
CAIAPHAS  Another change of wind. — What do you mean?
Are you this Man's disciple, Yes or No?
SAUL  Is it not written in our holy Law
That the Lord said to Moses, Send out men,
One man of every tribe, to spy the land?
CAIAPHAS  Well, what of that?
SAUL  And God, who leads men by a way they know not,
Sent me from Tarsus to spy out this Man.
NICODEMUS  A spy and self-confessed!
SAUL  Those spies came bringing from the brook of Eshcol
Clusters of mighty grapes, pomegranates, figs;
I bring you Dead Sea fruit, apples of Sodom.
CAIAPHAS  I cannot make out what you say.
NICODEMUS  The man is fortified in lunacy.
CAIAPHAS  I ask again, are you this Man's disciple?
SAUL  The hunter on the mountain stalks the hind,
The hawk pursues —

121

ANNAS Come down from your high mountain and talk sense.
Fathers, this man is no disciple.
He means — the thing is plainer than a post —
That he has watched the heretic; set himself
To watch Him closely and catch up His words;
This man can tell you the whole lying truth.
CAIAPHAS Then let him tell us; let the man speak plainly.
Come, witness, speak.
SAUL Caiaphas, Annas, Fathers of the Council,
I have your leave to speak and I will speak.
Though born in Tarsus, which is no mean city,
I am a man that am a Jew; for, know,
After the strictest sect of our religion
I was brought up a Pharisee —
CAIAPHAS You must not make a speech.
ANNAS Say what you said to me last night.
What does this Jesus say of us?
That is the point. Fathers, listen.
SAUL His word is in mine heart,
As a burning fire shut up within my bones,
And I am weary with forbearing.
ANNAS Stop quoting scripture and speak sense.
NICODEMUS Why must we listen to this ranting fellow?
ANNAS Come, tell us what He says of us.
SAUL Hypocrites!
ANNAS Ha, now we get the truth.
SAUL Blind leaders of the blind!
ANNAS We are blind leaders of the blind!
SAUL Whited sepulchres!
ANNAS You hear it? We are whited sepulchres.
You hear this truthful witness, what he says.
I knew that we would get the truth.
CAIAPHAS So we are whited sepulchres, hypocrites,
Blind leaders of the blind; is this the truth?
SAUL It is the truth.
CAIAPHAS He says these things of us?
SAUL These words with which I have defiled my mouth
Tickle the people's ears and make them laugh.

CAIAPHAS This is hot blasphemy.
ANNAS It is indeed;
Blaspheming us he blasphemes God.
CAIAPHAS What does the Council say?
ALL Blasphemy, blasphemy!
Let Him be sent for; we have heard enough.
NICODEMUS Caiaphas.
CAIAPHAS Silence! Let Nicodemus speak.
NICODEMUS Fathers, I wonder an old man like Annas
Should mock us in our holy Convocation
With this play-acting fellow. You heard him say
'I have defiled my mouth to speak these words';
But with what relish did he speak them! A witness?
Behind the false face of his evidence
The fellow leered at us; in shrewd pretence
Of holy zeal he plucked us by the beard.
Annas, if old in years, is young in wisdom
To be deceived by such a mocker. Why,
He owns himself a spy; you heard him own it;
And being so great a student of our Scripture
He quotes it to approve his vile profession.
You saw the serpent flick his double tongue,
'I am and I am not this Man's disciple';
You saw too how the serpent turned and twisted,
No one could catch his meaning. Look at him,
This man called Saul, whom God has sent from Tarsus,
This young man with a future —
No, do not blink at me and work your hands;
I know that they would clutch my throat. Listen!
Have you no fear of God to play this part,
To spy on this most righteous Man?
ANNAS Most righteous man! Listen to Nicodemus.
If Jesus is most righteous, what are we
But hypocrites, blind leaders of the blind?
CAIAPHAS Order, order!
I rule that we are finished with this witness.
You, Saul of Tarsus, leave the Council.
ANNAS But wait outside the door.

(SAUL OF TARSUS *goes out*)

CAIAPHAS  You have a witness, Nicodemus.
ANNAS  Why need he call another witness in?
Let Nicodemus call himself as witness.
CAIAPHAS  Himself?
ANNAS  Why not?
Am I in order if I ask a question?
CAIAPHAS  What is your question?
ANNAS  I ask of Nicodemus —
CAIAPHAS  What?
ANNAS  Is he too a disciple of the Man?
CAIAPHAS  Let Nicodemus answer if he will.
NICODEMUS  The question — does not seem — in order.
ANNAS  No, it is not; it is far out of order
That I should need to ask it. Caiaphas,
I, who am old in years and young in wisdom,
Think I can gauge the feeling of the Council.
If Nicodemus will not speak himself,
We will not hear his mouthpiece.
CAIAPHAS  Are you agreed?
ALL  Agreed, agreed.
ANNAS  I made a motion — it was seconded —
That Jesus be sent for and brought before us.
Is it not time you put it to the meeting?
CAIAPHAS  I put that motion to the meeting —
NICODEMUS  Wait!
CAIAPHAS  Well, we are waiting.
NICODEMUS  No; put the motion.
CAIAPHAS  All those in favour?
ALL  Agreed, agreed.
CAIAPHAS  Go, constables, and bring the Man before us,
The Man called Jesus; if He will not come,
Bring Him by force.
A CONSTABLE  Here is a crowd and with them a mad fellow
Who dances as he walks; they all are crying,
'A miracle, a miracle.'
ANNAS  Why, this may be the mystagogue Himself.

CAIAPHAS  Hold back the people.
CONSTABLES  Back, back; stand back, stand back.
CAIAPHAS  What do they want? Let one man speak.
CONSTABLES  What do you want? Let one man speak.
CAIAPHAS  What do they say?
A CONSTABLE  They say they bring a miracle to show you.
CAIAPHAS  A miracle? What kind of miracle?
A CONSTABLE  A man; the dancing fellow.
CAIAPHAS  Then bring this dancing fellow in before us;
But keep the others back.

(*The* BLIND MAN *enters*)

CAIAPHAS  Who are you?
BLIND MAN  Truly the light is sweet and a pleasant thing
It is for a blind man to see the sun.
Where is the sun? I cannot see the sun.
O friends, I hope I have not lost the sun.
ANNAS  This man is drunk.
NICODEMUS  No, no, he is not drunk. Look, Caiaphas,
I call you all to look; this man was blind
And now you see his eyes are open.
ANNAS  A trick, a trick! The man was never blind.
NICODEMUS  But I have seen him begging.
ANNAS  Why, any man can shut his eyes and cry,
'An alms, an alms, pity the blind.' A kick
Is all the miracle such fellows need
To give them sight enough to skip.
CAIAPHAS  Go, constables, and bring the Man called Jesus;
As for this fellow, leave him here with us.
BLIND MAN  Good constables, go bring the Man called Jesus;
That Jesus is the Man that I would see.
CAIAPHAS  That you would see, you, fellow?
BLIND MAN  And why should I not see? Have I not sight?
My eyes were dead, but they are living now.
O I can see so much I scarcely know
If I am here or there or where I am.
I see so many things that I would need
A hundred hands to tell me what they are.

125

I see you there; I see you seeing me;
You are the Sanhedrin, High Priest and all;
The holy men. God tells me you are men,
Or else I should not know it.

CAIAPHAS Constables, stop staring at this man and go.

( *The* CONSTABLES *go out* )

BLIND MAN Go, constables; no, stay and take me with you.
Where are you, constables? God curse these eyes;
Why do I stumble when I try to walk?
I must be blind again to see my way.

ANNAS I say the man is drunk.

BLIND MAN Ho, ho; a voice says I am drunk. Who spoke?
I have been often drunk; God pity me,
But what else would He have a blind man be?
But not to-day; no, I am worse than drunk;
To-day I have my sight and see.

ANNAS You have been drinking at the Feast.

BLIND MAN O you are speaking; you with the long beard;
A holy man. Where are the prayers that drip
Like gravy from your beard? You look like God. —
But where is God? I had not thought of that.
Now I have eyes, I must see God as well.
Where is the Temple where they say He lives?
I used to know but now I have my sight
I lose my way.

CAIAPHAS Stay where you are.

BLIND MAN What, would you have a blind man not see God?
Why have I eyes then? Why should I not see Him?
Ha, ha, perhaps you have not seen God either.
Perhaps you frighten Him; I should not wonder;
Perhaps when you, the priests, go in the Temple
God scampers like a little careful mouse
And runs and hides Himself behind the curtains.
I must go to the Temple and see God.
Besides, now I remember, Jesus said
I must go to the priest and show myself.
He said it; I must go.

126

ANNAS  Here is the priest, the High Priest.
BLIND MAN  And here am I. Look well at me, High Priest;
The people praise me as a miracle,
And so I am. Lift up your voice in prayer;
Offer a prayer of gladness and thanksgiving.
I know that you can pray;
I know by your long beard and scowling face.
How could a poor blind beggar pray himself?
CAIAPHAS  Be quiet, fellow.
BLIND MAN  I will be quiet; I do not want to speak;
When I have sight, why should I want to speak?
CAIAPHAS  Now listen to the question of the Council;
Do you say this Man, Jesus, gave you sight?
BLIND MAN  I say He made the clay, as God made Adam,
And laid it on my eyes and gave me sight.
CAIAPHAS  You say that to the Council?
BLIND MAN  No, no; I do not say it; I am dumb;
A poor dumb beggar who can only see.
Where is the door? The light must be the door.
My eyes are tired; my eyes are tired with seeing;
O I must close them and be blind again.
Where are you, friends? Here is your miracle.
Jesus and God, I have a lot to see.

(*The* BLIND MAN *goes out, and the people cry,* 'A miracle,
a miracle!')

CAIAPHAS  Bring back that man. Where are the constables?

(*The* CONSTABLES *enter*)

A CONSTABLE  Here, here; shall we bring back the miracle?
ANNAS  Be careful, Caiaphas;
The people count him as a miracle.
CAIAPHAS  No, let him go. Bring in the Man called Jesus.
Where is He? Why, fools, are you dumb?
Have you not brought Him?
Why do you stand there shuffling on your feet?
Is this another miracle?
A CONSTABLE  We went to take Him —

CAIAPHAS Well, did you not take Him?
A CONSTABLE But no man ever spoke as that Man speaks.
His words were living things, part of Himself;
They were an arm stretched out to hold us back.
NICODEMUS O Caiaphas, let me fill up the silence.
I see you staring at these men; they say
That no man ever spoke as that Man speaks.
You think that they are foolish ignorant men;
But what if I, a member of the Council,
As having spoken with the Man myself,
Should say the same, that no man ever spoke
As that Man speaks, what would you say?
ANNAS Nothing; there is no need to say. From now
We know you, Nicodemus; this Man too;
The thing is plain as a whitewashed sepulchre;
I say this Jesus must be put to death.
NICODEMUS Our Law can judge no man before it hear him.
ANNAS He has resisted our authority;
I at the proper time will vote for death.
He is as good as dead. You, Nicodemus,
Are you too His disciple? Why then, go
And buy some unguent to anoint His body;
The Man is dead already.
NICODEMUS Caiaphas, I protest.
ANNAS I know my words have the cold sound of death
In Nicodemus' ears; and why is that?
Have I not said, he too is a disciple?
If he is not, he needs only to say it.
We know this Man's disciples who they are,
A pack of fishermen from Galilee;
Can any good come out of Galilee?
Tax-gatherers and other publicans,
And wicked women too. Come, Nicodemus,
You are this Man's disciple, are you not? —
Fathers, you hear his silence?
NICODEMUS I say again
Our Law can judge no man before it hear him.
ANNAS He shouts so loud that you can hear his silence;

Jesus is dead and buried in that silence.
Fathers, let us be joyful. Hark, the music!
Here is a happy ending to our Council.
The flutes are playing in the Temple court.
The night grows brighter as the day grows darker,
Young priests have climbed and lit the Candelabra.
The people sing and join the holy dance;
You hear their voices lifted in the psalm,
And God can hear the shuffling of their feet.
See how the gold light treads across the chamber;
Come, let us join the dance. But wait;
Let Caiaphas first close the meeting.

CAIAPHAS Is it your will I close the meeting?

ALL Agreed, agreed.

CAIAPHAS Then let us pray.
Praised be Thou, Lord, who bestowest abundant grace and rememberest the promises to the fathers, and bringest a redeemer to their children's children, for Thy name's sake, out of love. O God, who bringest help and salvation, and art a shield, praised be Thou, O shield of Abraham. Amen.

ALL Amen.

ANNAS Fathers, step out; I too will shake my beard,
Joining the people in the holy dance;
Come, Nicodemus,
And dance as David danced before the Ark,
No Michal looks out through her lattice window.
The Spirit of the Lord lifts up our steps.
You, foolish constables, can dance as well;
But close the door behind.

( *The Members of the Council dance out with slow swinging movement, singing the hymn.* NICODEMUS *remains behind*)

He will not suffer thy foot to be moved: and he that keepeth thee will not sleep.

Behold, he that keepeth Israel: shall neither slumber nor sleep.

The Lord himself is thy keeper: the Lord is thy defence upon thy right hand;

So that the sun shall not burn thee by day: neither the moon by night.

The Lord shall preserve thee from all evil: yea, it is even he that shall keep thy soul.

The Lord shall preserve thy going out, and thy coming in: from this time forth for evermore.

(*The* CONSTABLES *close the door behind them*)


PRELUDE III

JOHN *sitting as before writing his Gospel.*

JOHN (*writing*) For these things were done, that the scripture should be fulfilled. A bone of him shall not be broken. And again another scripture saith, They shall look on him whom they pierced. And after this Joseph of Arimathea, being a disciple of Jesus, but secretly for fear of the Jews, besought Pilate that he might take away the body of Jesus: and Pilate gave him leave. He came therefore, and took the body of Jesus. And there came also Nicodemus, which at the first came to Jesus by night, and brought a mixture of myrrh and aloes, about an hundred pound weight.

About an hundred pound! Why, Mary's gift
Was but a pound, and Judas thought it costly,
And that was to anoint His living feet;
And this, an hundred pound of myrrh and aloes
Was to embalm His body for a night,
One night, for Jesus was no sleeping Pharaoh.
My lamp burns down;
The flame lies on the oil and soon will die;
And this old body that grows cold with time
Has no more life left than that floating flame.
How different was it on that Easter morning,
That first of Easters;
We raced together to the sepulchre,
Peter and I, and I outran my friend.

130

But Peter has outrun me in the end;
His course is finished, he has gained the crown.
James too and brother Paul and all of them
Have left me far behind. I am the last.
Yet not so far behind; no, not far now;
I run a race where old age outruns youth;
My weakness is my strength, my slowness speed,
And I am hastening on towards the mark.
How strange I am the last,
The only one now living on the earth
Who saw and talked with Jesus as a friend.
If I should die, would He not die again?
No, He will live still in His living Church. —
I must be writing. But I cannot see
By this small dying flame.
Caius may be awake still; I will ring. —
So Nicodemus, the same who came by night,
Came with his hundred pound of myrrh and aloes;
Alas, he came too late.

    (*An* ANGEL *enters*)

ANGEL  You struck the bell.
JOHN  But who are you?
ANGEL  I am the one who rolled away the stone.
JOHN  The stone?
ANGEL  I rolled it from the sepulchre; God said,
'Go, take an earthquake, roll away the stone.'
JOHN  Are you a servant of the house?
ANGEL  I am the angel of the sepulchre.
JOHN  An angel!
ANGEL  Body and clothes are one material;
I put them on just now outside the door.
Give me your hand, for you must come with me.
JOHN  You come to take me? I must die to-night?
ANGEL  To-night: some other night; it is the same.
JOHN  I think you are God's angel; it would not matter
Though you were not; you could not take me far.
I see that I must die.

Well, I will go with you; here is my hand.
But this is not like dying; though I am old.
How can I die when I am still alive?
ANGEL  No, you mistake me; this is not your hour.
It was another died to-night.
JOHN  Another of us martyred?
ANGEL  Nicodemus.
JOHN  Nicodemus!
ANGEL  Killed by the Jews; his spirit fled to heaven;
I met him on the way.
JOHN  O God be praised! You came to tell me that?
ANGEL  I came to tell you that; I also came
To lead you back through fifty years and more
To that dark morning at the sepulchre
And show you something Nicodemus saw;
Though Mary and the women went there early
He was the first.
JOHN  He told us nothing.
ANGEL  It was forbidden him to speak;
For once when he might have spoken he was silent.
Hold fast my hand and we are there.


SCENE III

*Outside the Sepulchre.*

( *Two* CONSTABLES *stand at the door. Two other* CONSTABLES *enter*)

1ST CONSTABLE  Halt! Who goes there?
3RD CONSTABLE  The Temple guard.
1ST CONSTABLE  Then pass the word.
3RD CONSTABLE  May angels guard the constables.
1ST CONSTABLE  Why are you so late in relieving us?
3RD CONSTABLE  We came the moment that the captain sent us.
Is this the sepulchre?
1ST CONSTABLE  Did you hear music on the way?
3RD CONSTABLE  We heard the soldiers singing in the castle.

1ST CONSTABLE  But afterwards; here in the garden?
3RD CONSTABLE  We heard the nightingales.
1ST CONSTABLE  That is not music. No, music in the air,
High in the air; sounds without instruments,
Voices without people, as though the air
Were playing of itself and singing too.
3RD CONSTABLE  No, we heard no such music.
1ST CONSTABLE  We are well quit of it;
It sounded too like heaven for my taste.
Good night and a safe watch.
3RD CONSTABLE  Good night and a sound sleep.

( *The first Two* CONSTABLES *go out*)

4TH CONSTABLE  What is this music in the air?
3RD CONSTABLE  They must have dreamt it.
4TH CONSTABLE  They would not sleep on guard.
3RD CONSTABLE  They would not sleep — do you think that,
    young friend?
Why does the captain set us two and two,
Except that one should sleep and one should wake?
We will take turns; and I will sleep first.
But pass the cider.
4TH CONSTABLE  The bottle is three-quarters empty.
3RD CONSTABLE  That is their music in the air.
I will hear music too, music for nothing.
Good health, a long life, and fat purse.
4TH CONSTABLE  I am too cold to sleep; it is the dew.
They say dew falls; I never felt it fall;
I think it rises from the ground.
3RD CONSTABLE  It is the heat that makes the dew.
4TH CONSTABLE  How can heat make the dew? The dew is
    cold.
3RD CONSTABLE  I do not know. I wish I were a dog,
That wakes and listens while he's still asleep.
4TH CONSTABLE  It will be morning in an hour.
Do you remember —
3RD CONSTABLE  Remember what?
4TH CONSTABLE  The day they sent us to arrest Him?

3RD CONSTABLE The Council? I remember.

4TH CONSTABLE And we came back without Him;
And we could only stand and tell the Council
That no one ever spoke as that Man spoke.

3RD CONSTABLE Death was a better constable.

4TH CONSTABLE I did not think He would be crucified.

3RD CONSTABLE He went about it the right way.

4TH CONSTABLE Perhaps He lies there on the shelf and listens.

3RD CONSTABLE But He is dead.

4TH CONSTABLE A dead man lies so still he seems to listen.
The dead are far more cunning than the living;
I think too that they have the sharper hearing,
Although they never will let on they hear.

3RD CONSTABLE He could not hear us from behind the stone.

4TH CONSTABLE Perhaps a spirit can pass through a stone.

3RD CONSTABLE A stone would be an open door to spirits,
If there were spirits.

4TH CONSTABLE You think there are no spirits?

3RD CONSTABLE No, there are none.

4TH CONSTABLE But if there are no spirits, why do you say
A stone would be an open door to spirits?

3RD CONSTABLE Because I speak of nothing.

4TH CONSTABLE But if there were no spirits, how could you
    say
There are no spirits?

3RD CONSTABLE In the same way that I can speak of nothing.

4TH CONSTABLE To speak of nothing would be not to speak;
If you can speak of spirits, there are spirits.
Listen, Listen!

3RD CONSTABLE I hear it.

4TH CONSTABLE The music in the air.

*(A hymn is heard in the distance)*

I bless the Lord because he doth
    by counsel me conduct:
And in the seasons of the night
    my reins do me instruct.

Because of this my heart is glad,
    and joy shall be exprest,
Ev'n by my glory; and my flesh
    in confidence shall rest.

Because my soul in grave to dwell
    shall not be left by thee;
Nor wilt thou give thine Holy One
    corruption to see.

Thou wilt show me the path of life;
    of joys there is full store
Before thy face; at thy right hand
    are pleasures evermore.

4TH CONSTABLE Angels, angels!
Were these not angels singing?
3RD CONSTABLE They were not jackals or hyænas.
4TH CONSTABLE Perhaps they sing because of Jesus.
3RD CONSTABLE They do not sing because of us.
4TH CONSTABLE What shall we do?
3RD CONSTABLE We cannot cheer them as we cheer a circus
And ask for it again, no, certainly.
4TH CONSTABLE We must do something; they were angels.
3RD CONSTABLE Go and arrest them then.
4TH CONSTABLE Shall we report it to the captain?
3RD CONSTABLE Why not report it to the priest?
Come, take a drink of cider; you will feel better;
Let me drink first. Health to the angels,
Though no need to wish immortals a long life.

( *The* BLIND MAN *enters with a sack*)

BLIND MAN I come in time; leave some for me, good friend.
3RD CONSTABLE Halt, who goes there?
BLIND MAN I halt; and why should I not halt?
I have come fast enough. You, sack, lie there;
O how the earth smells sweet, struck by the sack;
It smells of flowers and roses.

3RD CONSTABLE The dancing fellow!

BLIND MAN The singing constables! I heard you sing.
Who would have thought you had such pleasant voices?
Or did you bring the Temple choir? Where are they?

3RD CONSTABLE What have you in the sack?

BLIND MAN It might afflict your noses. Myrrh and aloes;
Surely it stinks enough. It makes the place
Smell like the holy Temple. Bees will wake
And come and sting us. A hundred pound;
Lift it; a hundred pound of precious smell.
Samson could not have carried it. O I
Shall stink of it for ever. I am a garden;
A sweet herb-border like the Shulamite.
I shall not need to die; I am embalmed
Like an Egyptian mummy. But tell me, friends,
Is this the sepulchre of Jesus?

3RD CONSTABLE What is His sepulchre to you?

BLIND MAN Why, surely, you are the wise constables
To ask what is His sepulchre to me.
Did you not know this Jesus gave me sight?
For how could I have known that I was blind
Unless He gave me sight?
Perhaps it was His own sight that He gave me;
He lies so blind there in the sepulchre.

3RD CONSTABLE Why have you come here?

BLIND MAN To see you, constables; was that not right?
Now I have eyes I must see all I can.
My eyes are blest to see such men as you.

3RD CONSTABLE We know you; you are one of His disciples;
We saw you at the Council: the dancing fellow.

BLIND MAN And I saw you; they sent you to arrest Him;
Why was it that you did not bring Him back?

3RD CONSTABLE Are you not His disciple?

BLIND MAN Why should you think it?

3RD CONSTABLE He gave you sight.

BLIND MAN Why did He give me sight? Come, tell me that.
Why did He take away my livelihood?
When I was blind, could I not eat and drink?
I did not need to close my eyes to sleep.

136

I had no sins; a blind man cannot sin.
Earth was a heaven that I could not see
And men who had their sight were walking angels
Or devils when they cursed me.

3RD CONSTABLE Why have you brought this sack?

BLIND MAN That sack, too, is a problem; I must work;
I must do this and that for Nicodemus;
You see I have to work both day and night;
I am a servant.

3RD CONSTABLE Servant to Nicodemus?

BLIND MAN Why not? He is a good man, Nicodemus,
Although he makes a blind man work for money.
And he is kind; I think he pities me,
Now I have lost my blindness.

3RD CONSTABLE Why have you come?

BLIND MAN It is this dead Man in the sepulchre
That I would speak to, if He is alive.
Jesus, Jesus, wake up and answer me,
Why did you take away a poor man's blindness?
Was I not a great blessing to the city,
Stirring the spirit of alms-giving?
Misers have wept to see me. Now, alas,
For want of a blind beggar to give alms to
The rich must die and go to hell.

4TH CONSTABLE He mocks the dead.

3RD CONSTABLE Or he is mocking us.

4TH CONSTABLE I think he plays for time.

3RD CONSTABLE It is some trick, we must arrest him.

BLIND MAN Wake up, and save me from the constables;
Make them as blind as the vile men of Sodom
Who wandered round the door.

3RD CONSTABLE Come, we arrest you, fellow.

BLIND MAN Leave go, leave go!

3RD CONSTABLE Come, come.

BLIND MAN Well, have you got me fast; what will you do?

3RD CONSTABLE How can we tie him up?

4TH CONSTABLE We passed a vineyard; I could smell the
blossoms;

137

The young vine-shoots would tie him safe enough;
It is close by.

3RD CONSTABLE Then go and pull them.

4TH CONSTABLE This eel will wriggle from your hands.

3RD CONSTABLE Then let us take him with us.

4TH CONSTABLE We cannot leave the sepulchre.

3RD CONSTABLE We shall not be long gone.

BLIND MAN Hold, I must wait for Nicodemus here.

3RD CONSTABLE When you are tied up you will wait the
better.

(*The Two* CONSTABLES *go out with the* BLIND MAN.
NICODEMUS *enters*)

NICODEMUS O Jesus, if your spirit haunts this place —
I feel that you are here, here in this garden,
Where they have brought and planted your poor body,
But not to rise again — forgive, forgive me!
You see me kneeling here, my sin as dark
As the black shadows of this moon-washed garden.
I tried and yet I did not try to save you;
Something I said and yet I did not speak.
O had I spoken boldly, or even said
'I am this man's disciple,' I do not think
They would have dared to do what they have done.
My silence was the witness that condemned you.
I was afraid; afraid of nothing, for me
They could not crucify as they did you.
I was afraid of nothing but to speak,
Afraid to tell them what they knew. That silence
Became a weight upon my lips, a chain
That bound me, a dumb devil that afflicted me;
And now it is become a wilderness
Where I must ever wander and be lost.
I thought that you would save yourself at last;
I thought — O God, I even thought — that day —
Only two days ago — when I went out
And looked towards the crowd at Calvary
And saw you stand above the people's heads

138

That you had saved yourself — and then I knew
It was the cross that held you in its arms.
I come again by night; but now too late,
For I can only come to your dead body.
This is a vain work that I come about,
Bringing this useless load of myrrh and aloes;
For to embalm your body with these unguents
Is to perpetuate the wounds and blood.
It is your death that I would keep alive;
And it was I who crucified you, I
Who might have spoken and did not speak.
Forgive me, Lord. Why do I call you Lord?
Is it that in some majesty of death
Your spirit has grown greater than a man's?
Or was it always so, and now in death
I know you, what you are?
Lord, Lord, forgive me, Lord!

(*The Two* CONSTABLES *enter with the* BLIND MAN *bound*)

3RD CONSTABLE Here is another at the sepulchre.
BLIND MAN Nicodemus!
NICODEMUS What, is that you?
BLIND MAN The constables have taken me.
NICODEMUS Leave go my servant. Who are you?
3RD CONSTABLE The Temple Guard.
NICODEMUS Why are you here?
3RD CONSTABLE We watch the sepulchre.
NICODEMUS Well, I commend your watching; but this man,
He came here at my bidding. Set him free.
BLIND MAN I told you, fools.

(*The* CONSTABLES *unbind the* BLIND MAN)

NICODEMUS You constables, come here and lend a hand;
I want the stone rolled from the sepulchre.
3RD CONSTABLE We have no orders from the captain.
NICODEMUS Take them from me, then.
3RD CONSTABLE We were sent here to guard the body.
NICODEMUS I do not come to steal but to embalm.

Come, help my servant to roll back the stone.

4TH CONSTABLE The music in the air!

NICODEMUS What is that music?

4TH CONSTABLE It is created music, made from nothing.

(*A hymn is heard from the air*)

> Ye gates, lift up your heads on high;
> ye doors that last for aye,
> Be lifted up, that so the King
> of glory enter may.

> But who of glory is the King?
> the mighty Lord is this;
> Ev'n that same Lord, that great in might
> and strong in battle is.

> Ye gates, lift up your heads; ye doors,
> doors that do last for aye,
> Be lifted up, that so the King
> of glory enter may.

> But who is he that is the King
> of glory? who is this?
> The Lord of hosts, and none but he
> the King of glory is.

(*An earthquake, with thunder and lightning*)

BLIND MAN O master, master, look! the earth is drunk;
It is not I this time.
The earth is turned to sea; we rock like boats;
It gives me a cold rising stomach.

NICODEMUS This is an earthquake.

BLIND MAN The constables are shipwrecked; they have fallen.

NICODEMUS Kneel down, kneel down.

BLIND MAN O master, I am frightened.
The ground is rising up to swallow me.

NICODEMUS Look at the stone, the stone!

BLIND MAN What stone?

NICODEMUS There at the sepulchre; it moves.

BLIND MAN O God, the stone is frightened too.

NICODEMUS It trembles like a curtain.

BLIND MAN It will fall back and crush us.

NICODEMUS Look! it is rolling like a wheel.
The light, the light!

(*A lighted Altar is disclosed*)

BLIND MAN O master, is this heaven? am I dead?

NICODEMUS The tomb is full of light.

BLIND MAN Or am I blind again to see this sight?
Only the blind could see it.

NICODEMUS Light, light; nothing but light;
The tomb is empty; He is gone.

BLIND MAN Where is He gone? Go in the tomb and look;
He may be there.

NICODEMUS The Lord is risen.

BLIND MAN But He was dead; could the earthquake wake
Him?

NICODEMUS Waken these sleeping men; they too must see it.

BLIND MAN Waken, waken! They will not waken;
They seem alive and dead at the same time.

NICODEMUS Then let them lie; this sight is not for them.

BLIND MAN But where is Jesus? Call on Him;
If He is gone, He cannot have gone far.

NICODEMUS Go, leave me here.

BLIND MAN Go where?

NICODEMUS Back to Jerusalem.

BLIND MAN He may be going there.

NICODEMUS Go quickly; I will follow soon.

BLIND MAN I am afraid to meet Him, a dead man;
He may come walking to me through the trees;
I wish I never had received my sight.

(*The* BLIND MAN *goes out*)

NICODEMUS O risen Lord,
I do not ask you to forgive me now;
There is no need.

141

I came to-night to speak to your dead body,
To touch it with my hands and say 'Forgive,'
For though I knew it could not speak to me
Or even hear, yet it was once yourself;
It is dissolved and risen like a dew,
And now I know,
As dawn forgives the night, as spring the winter,
You have forgiven me. It is enough.
Why do I kneel before your empty tomb?
You are not here, for you are everywhere;
The grass, the trees, the air, the wind, the sky,
Nothing can now refuse to be your home;
Nor I. Lord, live in me and I shall live.
This is the word you spoke,
The whole earth hears it, for the whole earth cries,

I AM THE RESURRECTION, AND THE LIFE: HE THAT BELIEVETH IN
ME THOUGH HE WERE DEAD, YET SHALL HE LIVE: AND WHO-
SOEVER LIVETH AND BELIEVETH IN ME SHALL NEVER DIE.

## The Chalk-Cliff

Blasted and bored and undermined
   By quarrying seas
Reared the erect chalk-cliff with black flints lined.
   (Flints drop like nuts from trees
When the frost bites
The chalk on winter nights.)

Save for frail shade of jackdaw's flight
   No night was there,
But blue-skyed summer and a cliff so white
   It stood like frozen air;
Foot slipped on damp
Chalk where the limpets camp.

With only purple of sea-stock
   And jackdaw's shade
To mitigate that blazing height of chalk
   I stood like a soul strayed
In paradise
Hiding my blinded eyes.

## The Ventriloquists

The birds sang in the rain
    That rhythmically waving its grey veil
From smoking hill-top flowed to misty plain,
    Where one white house shone sharply as a sail;

But not so bright as these,
    The anemones that held the wood snow-bound,
The water-drops waiting to fall from trees,
    The rusty catkins crawling on the ground.

March buds give little shelter;
    Better seek shelter in the open rain
Than where tree-gathered showers fall helter-skelter,
    I meditated; but 'Turn, turn again,'

The birds shrieked through their song;
    So rooted to the leaf-soft earth I stood,
Letting my restless eye wander among
    The thick sky-scrawling branches of the wood.

But no bird could I see
    In criss-cross of thin twigs or sudden twists
Where branching tree interrupted branching tree;
    Yet everywhere those hidden ventriloquists

Were singing in the wood,
    Flinging their cheating voices here and there;
But seeing nothing though I walked or stood
    I thought the singing grew out of the air.

## August

The cows stood in a thunder-cloud of flies,
    As lagging through the field with trailing feet
I kicked up scores of skipper butterflies
    That hopped a little way, lazy with heat.

The wood I found was in deep shelter sunk,
    Though bryony leaves shone with a glossy sweat
And creeping over ground and up tree-trunk
    The ivy in the sun gleamed bright and wet.

Songs brief as Chinese poems the birds sung
    And insects of all sheens, blue, brown and yellow,
Darted and twisted in their flight and hung
    On air that groaned like hoarse sweet violoncello.

No leaf stirred in the wood-discouraged wind,
    But foliage hung on trees, like heavy wigs;
The sun, come from the sky, was close behind
    The fire-fringed leaves and in among the twigs.

# Autumn Seeds

Although a thoughtful bee still travels
And midge-ball ravels and unravels,
Yet strewn along the pathway lie
Like small open sarcophagi
The hazel-nuts broken in two
And cobwebs catch the seed-pearl dew.

Now summer's flowers are winter's weeds,
I think of all the sleeping seeds;
Winds were their robins and by night
Frosts glue their leafy cover tight;
Snow may shake down its dizzy feathers,
They will sleep safely through all weathers.

## Snow

Ridged thickly on black bough
  And foaming on twig-fork in swollen lumps
At flirt of bird-wing or wind's sough
  Plump snow tumbled on snow softly with sudden dumps.

Where early steps had made
  A wavering track through the white-blotted road
Breaking its brightness with blue shade,
  Snow creaked beneath my feet with snow heavily shod.

I reached a snow-thatched rick
  Where men sawed bedding off for horse and cow;
There varnished straws were lying thick
  Paving with streaky gold the trodden silver snow.

Such light filled me with awe
  And nothing marred my paradisal thought,
That robin least of all I saw
  Lying too fast asleep, his song choked in his throat.

## The Missel-Thrush

That missel-thrush
Scorns to alight on a low bush,
And as he flies
And tree-top after tree-top tries,
His shadow flits
And harmlessly on tree-trunk hits.

Shutting his wings
He sways and sings and sways and sings,
And from his bough
As in deep water he looks through
He sees me there
Crawl at the bottom of the air.


## The Chalk-Quarry

A solitary yew,
    Fern-haired and ruddy-thewed,
That light with no sharp needle can prick through,
    Itself makes a small forest in the wood.

The strong sun darkening still
    That yew's *memento mori*
Fills with a fiercer light out on the hill
    The open sepulchre of the old chalk-quarry.

## South Downs

No water cries among these hills,
  The mist hides and enlarges,
Though rain in every road-rut spills
  Where leaves have sunk their barges.

No freshet in a hollow brake
  Utters its shy cold fears,
Only the chiming sheep-bells make
  One Sabbath of the years.

## Cuckoo in May

Cuckoo that like a cuckoo-clock
Calls out the hours so fast,
Days, months and years go slipping past,
O for a while be dumb
Lest in a moment I become
Old as that man I stopped to watch
And chat with in my morning walk,
His back as rounded as a hoop,
Who did not need to stoop
To pull out weeds in his potato-patch.

## The Elm Beetle

So long I sat and conned
That naked bole
With the strange hieroglyphics scored
That those small priests,
The beetle-grubs, had bored,
Telling of gods and kings and beasts
And the long journey of the soul
Through magic-opened gates
To where the throned Osiris waits,
That when at last I woke
I stepped from an Egyptian tomb
To see the wood's sun-spotted gloom,
And rising cottage smoke
That leaned upon the wind and broke,
Roller-striped fields, and smooth cow-shadowed pond.

## Walking in Beech Leaves

I tread on many autumns here
    But with no pride,
For at the leaf-fall of each year
    I also died.

This is last autumn, crisp and brown,
    That my knees feel;
But through how many years sinks down
    My sullen heel.

## February

So thick a mist darkened the day
Not two trees distant flew my friend, the jay,
    To keep love's angry tryst
    Somewhere in the damp mist,
    And as I brushed each bush
    Rain-buds fell in a rush,
One might have said it rained,
While green buds on the barer boughs remained.

But where with looped and twisted twine
Wild clematis, bryony and woodbine
    And such reptilian growth
    Hung in decaying sloth,
    I stood still thinking how
    Two months or three from now
The green buds would not tarry
More than those flashing drops of February.

# The Echoing Cliff

White gulls that sit and float
Each on his shadow like a boat,
Sandpipers, oystercatchers
And herons, those grey stilted watchers,
From loch and corran rise,
And as they scream and squawk abuse
Echo from wooded cliff replies
So clearly that the dark pine boughs,
Where goldcrests flit
And owls in drowsy wisdom sit,
Are filled with sea-birds and their cries.

# The Scarecrow

He strides across the grassy corn
That has not grown since it was born,
A piece of sacking on a pole,
A ghost, but nothing like a soul.

Why must this dead man haunt the spring
With arms anxiously beckoning?
Is spring not hard enough to bear
For one at autumn of his year?

## The Mountain

The burn ran blacker for the snow
And ice-floe on ice-floe
Jangled in heavy lurches
Beneath the claret-coloured birches.

Dark grouse rose becking from the ground
And deer turned sharp heads round,
The antlers on their brows
Like stunted trees with withered boughs.

I climbed to where the mountain sloped
And long wan bubbles groped
Under the ice's cover,
A bridge that groaned as I crossed over.

I reached the mist, brighter than day,
That showed a specious way
By narrow crumbling shelves,
Where rocks grew larger than themselves.

But when I saw the mountain's spire
Looming through that damp fire,
I left it still unwon
And climbed down to the setting sun.

# Man and Cows

I stood aside to let the cows
Swing past me with their wrinkled brows,
Bowing their heads as they went by
As to a woodland deity
To whom they turned mute eyes
To save them from the plaguing god of flies.

And I too cursed Beelzebub,
Watching them stop to rub
A bulging side or bony haunch
Against a trunk or pointing branch
And lift a tufted tail
To thresh the air with its soft flail.

They stumbled heavily down the slope,
As Hethor led them or the hope
Of the lush meadow-grass,
While I remained, thinking it was
Strange that we both were held divine,
In Egypt these, man once in Palestine.

## The Swallows

All day — when early morning shone
With every dewdrop its own dawn
And when cockchafers were abroad
Hurtling like missiles that had lost their road —

The Swallows twisting here and there
Round unseen corners of the air
Upstream and down so quickly passed
I wondered that their shadows flew as fast.

They steeple-chased over the bridge
And dropped down to a drowning midge
Sharing the river with the fish,
Although the air itself was their chief dish.

Blue-winged snowballs! until they turned
And then with ruddy breasts they burned;
All in one instant everywhere,
Jugglers with their own bodies in the air.

## The Thunderstorm

When Coniston Old Man was younger
And his deep-quarried sides were stronger,
Goats may have leapt about Goat's Water;
But why the tarn that looks like its young daughter
Though lying high under the fell
Should be called Blind Tarn, who can tell?

For from Dow Crag, passing it by,
I saw it as a dark presageful eye;
And soon I knew that I was not mistaken
Hearing the thunder the loose echoes waken
About Scafell and Scafell Pike
And feeling the slant raindrops strike.

And when I came to Walna Pass
Hailstones hissing and hopping among the grass,
Beneath a rock I found a hole;
But with sharp crack and rumbling roll on roll
So quick the lightning came and went
The solid rock was like a lighted tent.

## A Wet Day

Breasting the thick brushwood that hid my track
Diffuse wetness of rain had stained me black;
My clinging coat I hung on a bough-knop
And sodden shapeless hat I laid on top.

With heavy hat and coat left on the bough
I felt a snake that had cast off his slough
And joined the slow black slugs that strolled abroad
Making soft shameless love on the open road.

But, turning on my steps, startled I stood
To see a dead man hanging in the wood;
By two clear feet of air he swung afloat,
One who had hanged himself in hat and coat.

The cuckoo's double note
Loosened like bubbles from a drowning throat
Floats through the air
In mockery of pipit, lark and stare.

The stable-boys thud by
Their horses slinging divots at the sky
And with bright hooves
Printing the sodden turf with lucky grooves.

As still as a windhover
A shepherd in his flapping coat leans over
His tall sheep-crook
And shearlings, tegs and yoes cons like a book.

And one tree-crowned long barrow
Stretched like a sow that has brought forth her farrow
Hides a king's bones
Lying like broken sticks among the stones.

# Christmas Day

Last night in the open shippen
    The Infant Jesus lay,
While cows stood at the hay-crib
    Twitching the sweet hay.

As I trudged through the snow-fields
    That lay in their own light,
A thorn-bush with its shadow
    Stood doubled on the night.

And I stayed on my journey
    To listen to the cheep
Of a small bird in the thorn-bush
    I woke from its puffed sleep.

The bright stars were my angels
    And with the heavenly host
I sang praise to the Father,
    The Son and Holy Ghost.

# The Gramophone

We listened to your birds to-night
By the firelight,
The nightingales that trilled to us
From moonlit boughs.

Though golden snow-flakes from the gloom
Looked in the room,
Those birds' clear voices lingered on
Your gramophone.

'Good-night' we said and as I go
High-heeled with snow
I almost hope to hear one now
From a bare bough.

# The Archaeologist

Although men may dig up
A broken Bacchus with a vine-wreathed cup
Or helmeted chryselephantine goddess;
Though Aphrodite divine and godless,
Helped by a rope, rise from the sea,
None is immortal but Persephone.

See, by an English lane
Cold Hades lets her rise again.
In celandines that in a blaze
Spread like gold starfish their flat rays
Revisiting our earth and sky
Death's wife reveals her immortality.

She glitters with a light
That sharpens, as is said, the swallow's sight;
I am not like that twittering bird;
Too clear a memory my eyes has blurred;
Not this side heaven I'll see again
As once I saw it a gold English lane.

# The Falls of Glomach

Rain drifts forever in this place
Tossed from the long white lace
The Falls trail on black rocks below,
And golden-rod and rose-root shake
In wind that they forever make;
So though they wear their own rainbow
It's not in hope, but just for show,
For rain and wind together
Here through the summer make a chill wet weather.

# Glow-Worms

As though the dark had called
To chrysolite and emerald,
Earth brings out jewel by jewel,
Love stoking their bright fires, itself the fuel.

To flying beetles, 'Come,
Find here your children and your home,'
They sing with a green light,
Each glow-worm her own Venus in the night.

## Beaulieu River

Largest of Forest snakes, by heath and scrog
It stretches in its blue sky-borrowed coat,
For while its tail trails in a cotton bog
It grips with foaming mouth the Solent's throat.

## The Frogs

Each night that I come down the strath
Frogs turn heels-over-head,
And their white bellies on the path
Tell where to tread.

Of fox with brush above the brake
And kestrel pinned to air
And thin dark river of a snake
Let them beware!

Fat acrobats, I watch them turn
Kicking the evening dew,
Till in white waves that ride the burn
I see frogs too.

# The Dunes

These heavy hills of sand,
That marram-grasses bind
Lest they should fly off on the wind,
Hold back the sea from Sea-kings' Land.

Such a waste holds me too
From fields where shadows fly,
Wolds, woods and streams that quote the sky,
All the sweet country that is you.


# Long Meg and her Daughters

When from the Druid's Head I came
The low sun doubled tussock-tump
And half in shadow, half in flame
Stood the Stone Circle. Lump by lump
Viewing her daughters Long Meg said,
'Come, stranger, make your choice of one;
All are my children, stone of stone,
And none of them yet wed;
They wait to play at kiss-in-the-ring
With only now the wind to sing.'
But I, 'No, mother, all are fat
And some too old have fallen down flat.'
Meg frowned, 'You should be dead
To take instead a young tombstone to bed.'

## Hibernating Snails

Here where the castle faces south
The ivy spreading its flat tree
Hides snails in heaps thick and uncouth,
All fast asleep with open mouth,
Although they breathe no air,
Each china throat sealed up with glair;
Yet some will never wake at all,
For two years old or even three
They crawled alive to their own funeral.

## Nightfall on Sedgemoor

The darkness like a guillotine
    Descends on the flat earth;
The flocks look white across the rhine
    All but one lamb, a negro from its birth.

The pollards hold up in the gloom
    Knobbed heads with long stiff hair
That the wind tries to make a broom
    To sweep the moon's faint feather from the air.

What makes the darkness fall so soon
    Is not the short March day
Nor the white sheep nor brightening moon,
    But long June evenings when I came this way.


## A Prehistoric Camp

It was the time of year
    Pale lambs leap with thick leggings on
Over small hills that are not there,
    That I climbed Eggardon.

The hedgerows still were bare,
    None ever knew so late a year;
Birds built their nests in the open air,
    Love conquering their fear.

But there on the hill-crest,
    Where only larks or stars look down,
Earthworks exposed a vaster nest,
    Its race of men long flown.

166

## The Flesh-Scraper

If I had sight enough
Might I not find a finger-print
Left on this flint
By Neolithic man or Kelt?
So knapped to scrape a wild beast's pelt,
The thumb below, fingers above,
See, my hand fits it like a glove.


## Essex Salt-Marsh

Now the tide's task is done,
Marsh runnels turn and chuckling run
Or come to a standstill,
The level ground for them a breathless hill.

And as they run or faint
Through mud that takes the sunset's paint,
The gullies they have worn
Shine as with purple grapes and golden corn.

## Drought in the Fens

How often from the shade of trees
I thought of that rich man, Dives,
And how no diamond drop was given
To his or earth's cracked lips from heaven.

Green apples fell and lay around
As though they grew upon the ground,
And ditches, shrunk to muddy roads,
Starved limbless fish and man-legged toads.

So when the sand-walled flats I crossed
Hardened by heat as by a frost,
How strange it was that there could be
Still so much water in the sea.

## Morning in the Combe

The low sun halves the combe,
One side in sunlight, one in gloom,
And where they meet together
I walk from winter into summer weather.

There hard mud kept the cast
Of hoof and claw and foot that passed,
While here I stumble over
Moist earth that draws me backward like a lover.

## The Cuillin Hills

Each step a cataract of stones
So that I rise and sink at once,
Slowly up to the ridge I creep;
And as through drifting smoke
Of mist grey-black as a hoodie-crow
The ghostly boulders come and go
And two hoarse ravens croak
That hopped with flapping wings by a dead sheep,
All is so hideous that I know
It would not kill me though I fell
A thousand feet below;
On you, Black Cuillin, I am now in hell.

## Cuckoos

When coltsfoot withers and begins to wear
Long silver locks instead of golden hair,
And fat red catkins from black poplars fall
And on the ground like caterpillars crawl,
And bracken lifts up slender arms and wrists
And stretches them, unfolding sleepy fists,
The cuckoos in a few well-chosen words
Tell they give Easter eggs to the small birds.

## Climbing in Glencoe

The sun became a small round moon
And the scared rocks grew pale and weak
As mist surged up the col, and soon
So thickly everywhere it tossed
That though I reached the peak
With height and depth both lost
It might as well have been a plain;
Yet when, groping my way again,
On to the scree I stept
It went with me, and as I swept
Down its loose rumbling course
Balanced I rode it like a circus horse.

## Suilven

It rose dark as a stack of peat
With mountains at its feet,
Till a bright flush of evening swept
And on to its high shoulder leapt
And Suilven, a great ruby, shone;
And though that evening light is dead,
The mountain in my mind burns on,
As though I were the foul toad, said
To bear a precious jewel in his head.

## Mountain View

Can those small hills lying below
Be mountains that some hours ago
I gazed at from beneath?
Can such intense blue be the sea's
Or that long cloud the Hebrides?
Perhaps I prayed enough
By crawling up on hands and knees
The sharp loose screes,
Sweat dripping on the lichen's scurf,
And now in answer to my prayer
A vision is laid bare;
Or on that ledge, holding my breath,
I may have even slipped past Death.


## The Shepherd's Hut

Now when I could not find the road
Unless beside it also flowed
This cobbled beck that through the night,
Breaking on stones, makes its own light,

Where blackness in the starlit sky
Is all I know a mountain by,
A shepherd little thinks how far
His lamp is shining like a star.

## Children Gathering Violets

Children, small Herods, slay these Innocents
With blue untidy faces and sweet scents;
But violets gone or even autumn here
Spring in the children lasts through all the year.

## Walking in Mist

At first the river Noe
Like a snake's belly gleamed below,
And then in mist was lost;
The hill too vanished like a ghost
And all the day was gone
Except the damp grey light that round me shone.

From Lose Hill to Mam Tor,
Darkness behind me and before,
I gave the track its head;
But as I followed where it led,
That light went all the way
As though I made and carried my own day.

## Reflections on the River

Rose-petals fall without a touch
As though it were too much
I should be standing by,
And poplars in no wind at all
Keep swaying left and right
With the slow motion of their height
Beneath a small white cloud that soon
Will pluck light from the dark and be the moon.

But where roach rise and bite the Ouse
Round ripples spread out like the first
Drops of a storm about to burst
And in the water toss the boughs
And crack the garden wall;
And as I gaze down in the sky
I see the whole vault shake
As though the heavens were seized with an earthquake.

## *A Dead Mole*

Strong-shouldered mole,
That so much lived below the ground,
Dug, fought and loved, hunted and fed,
For you to raise a mound
Was as for us to make a hole;
What wonder now that being dead
Your body lies here stout and square
Buried within the blue vault of the air?

# Fields of Asparagus

From their long narrow beds
Asparagus raise reptilian heads
(Even the sand in May awakes)
And men who think that they are snakes
With shining knives
Walk to and fro, taking their scaly lives.

My path goes to the sea
But turning round comes back to me
In clouds of wind-blown sand
Making a desert of the land,
Where men must fight
With purple snakes that grow up in a night.

# Overtaken by Mist

Like lightning on the mountain-slope
The stalker's path zigzagged,
And climbing it with steps that lagged
I often raised my eyes in hope
To where Scour Ouran's head was bare;
But mist that gathered from nowhere
With a bright darkness filled the air,
Until, both earth and heaven gone,
Never was man or angel so alone.

## *Walking on the Cliff*

But for a sleepy gull that yawned
   And spread its wings and dropping disappeared
This evening would have dawned
   To the eternity my flesh has feared.

For too intent on a blackcap
   Perched like a miser on the yellow furze
High over Birling Gap,
   That sang 'Gold is a blessing not a curse,'

How near I was to stepping over
   The brink where the gull dropped to soar beneath.
While now safe as a lover
   I walk the cliff-edge arm in arm with Death.

## *Idleness*

God, you've so much to do,
To think of, watch and listen to,
That I will let all else go by
And lending ear and eye
Help you to watch how in the combe
Winds sweep dead leaves without a broom;
And rooks in the spring-reddened trees
Restore their villages,
Nest by dark nest
Swaying at rest on the trees' frail unrest;
Or on this limestone wall,
Leaning at ease, with you recall
How once these heavy stones
Swam in the sea as shells and bones;
And hear that owl snore in a tree
Till it grows dark enough for him to see;
In fact, will learn to shirk
No idleness that I may share your work.

# Autumn Mist

So thick a mist hung over all,
Rain had no room to fall;
It seemed a sea without a shore;
The cobwebs drooped heavy and hoar
As though with wool they had been knit;
Too obvious mark for fly to hit!

And though the sun was somewhere else
The gloom had brightness of its own
That shone on bracken, grass and stone
And mole-mound with its broken shells
That told where squirrel lately sat,
Cracked hazel-nuts and ate the fat.

And sullen haws in the hedgerows
Burned in the damp with clearer fire;
And brighter still than those
The scarlet hips hung on the briar
Like coffins of the dead dog-rose;
All were as bright as though for earth
Death were a gayer thing than birth.

## The Nightingale and Owl

How often had I tried to see
A nightingale, and only seen the tree;
To-night I went with new belief
That I should see one, looking leaf by leaf.

And I was glad too that I went,
For as I listened, drinking the may's scent,
Another came, drawn by the tale
Of that Greek girl changed to a nightingale.

O Philomela, but for me
Who frightened that dark shadow from the tree,
A further change you had gone through,
Your 'Tereu-tereu' not 'Too-whit too-whoo!'

## A Brimstone Butterfly

The autumn sun that rose at seven
Has risen again at noon,
Where the hill makes a later heaven,
And fringing with bright rainbow hair
The boughs that lace the sky
Has wakened half a year too soon
This brimstone butterfly,
That fluttering every way at once
Searches in vain the moss and stones, —
Itself the only primrose there.

## Ba Cottage

There at the watershed I turned
And looked back at the house I burned —
Burnt, too, by many another tramp
Who sought its shelter, dry or damp.

For coming from the mist-thick moor
I made the window-sill my door
And, wet incendiary, tore up wood
And fed the grate's wide mouth with food.

Then leaning on the mantelshelf
As though a mountain now myself
I smoked with mist and dripped with rain
That slowly made me dry again.

## Culbin Sands

Here lay a fair fat land;
  But now its townships, kirks, graveyards
Beneath bald hills of sand
  Lie buried deep as Babylonian shards.

But gales may blow again;
  And like a sand-glass turned about
The hills in a dry rain
  Will flow away and the old land look out;

And where now hedgehog delves
  And conies hollow their long caves
Houses will build themselves
  And tombstones rewrite names on dead men's graves.

## *After the Gale*

I pity trees that all their life
Have ivy for a wife
Or with dark mistletoe they bear
Keep Christmas through the year.

So seeing oak-twigs grow on thorn
Where they were never born,
And sprays of ash-keys and pine-cones
Grow on a briar at once.

I blamed the gale that through the night
Had with perverse delight
Quartered rich children on the poor
Like foundlings at their door.

## A Prospect of Death

If it should come to this
You cannot wake me with a kiss,
Think I but sleep too late
Or once again keep a cold angry state.

So now you have been told; —
I or my breakfast may grow cold,
But you must only say
'Why does he miss the best part of the day?'

Even then you may be wrong;
Through woods torn by a blackbird's song
My thoughts may often roam
While graver business makes me stay at home.

There will be time enough
To go back to the earth I love
Some other day that week,
Perhaps to find what all my life I seek.

So do not dream of danger;
Forgive my lateness or my anger;
You have so much forgiven,
Forgive me this or that, or Hell or Heaven.

# The Stone Eagles

Purple and gold and wet
   To Toller Fratrum, Wynyard Eagle,
Both roads in the sunset
   Shone with a light so rich and regal.
Which choose without regret?

Chance led me by the one
   Where two lean-headed eagles perched
Rain-pitted to the bone
   And the last dregs of daylight searched
With their blind eyes of stone.

What were they watching for?
   Wild eagles that again would fly
Over a waste land or
   Scything wide circles in the sky
Mechanic birds of war?

## Snow Harvest

The moon that now and then last night
Glanced between clouds in flight
Saw the white harvest that spread over
The stubble fields and even roots and clover.

It climbed the hedges, overflowed
And trespassed on the road,
Weighed down fruit-trees and when winds woke
From white-thatched roofs rose in a silver smoke.

How busy is the world to-day!
Sun reaps, rills bear away
The lovely harvest of the snow
While bushes weep loud tears to see it go.

## Passing the Graveyard

I see you did not try to save
The bouquet of white flowers I gave;
So fast they wither on your grave.

Why does it hurt the heart to think
Of that most bitter abrupt brink
Where the low-shouldered coffins sink?

These living bodies that we wear
So change by every seventh year
That in a new dress we appear.

Limbs, spongy brain and slogging heart,
No part remains the selfsame part;
Like streams they stay and still depart.

You slipped slow bodies in the past;
Then why should we be so aghast
You flung off the whole flesh at last?

Let him who loves you think instead
That like a woman who has wed
You undressed first and went to bed.

## In Moonlight

Rain pattered in the poplar trees,
    And yet there was no rain;
It was clear moon; the trees' unease
    Made me hear water plain.

It seemed that lover walked by lover
    So sharp my shadow showed;
We never needed to step over
    The tree-trunks on the road.

The moon too on the other side
    From tree to tree flew on,
As though she had forsook the tide
    For her Endymion.

The truest lovers I could have —
    So to myself I said —
The shadow marking out my grave
    And moon lending a spade.

# The Blind Children

Where caterpillars ate their fill
On hazels' mealy leaves until
The boughs were stript half-bare
And leaves hung riddled with clear holes of air,

I met with children who upturned
Faces to where the blue sky burned,
Some blinking in the glare,
Some looking up with a white open stare.

I did not need to question which
Should leave the road and take the ditch;
I felt it was small kindness
To children walking arm in arm in blindness.

From their blind eyes I borrowed sight
To see the leaves against the light
Rich and not ruinous,
Set with bright diamonds on the fire-fringed boughs.

## On the Hillside

What causes the surprise
That greets me here under the piecemeal skies
Of this thick-wooded scar?
Is it the look that the familiar
Keeps as of something strange
When so much else is constant but to change?
No, it's the thought that this white sun that cleaves
A silvery passage through the leaves
Is the same sun that cleft them
A week ago, as though I never left them
And never went in the sad interval
To my friend's funeral,
Though crossing the churchyard to-day I shivered
To see how fast on a fresh grave the flowers had withered.

## The Day Ends

The day ends and its heat
Lies in chill dews about our feet;
But though its twelve hours seemed as soon
Gone as the twelve strokes struck at noon,
So much those hours have freed
To blow away for memory's seed,
Will they not still be ours,
Fixed like the church-tower's gilt and holy hours?

## The Shower

The cherry-pickers left their picking
And ladders through the branches sticking
And cherries hung like gouts of blood
Down the long aisles of white-washed wood.

But now the sun is breaking through
Dark clouds that dry to pools of blue
And the smooth Medway lies uncreased
Except for drops the boughs released.

What is it makes the sun so proud
He will not suck a passing cloud
But needs raindrops to quench his thirst?
Well, let him do his picking first.


## At Formby

From that wide empty shore,
No foot had ever trod before
(Or since the sea drew back the tide),
I climbed the dune's soft slide
To where no higher than my hand
Wind-bitten pines grew in the clogging sand.

But farther from the beach
The trees rose up beyond my reach,
And as I walked, they still grew taller
And I myself smaller and smaller,
Till gazing up at a high wood
I felt that I had found my lost childhood.

# In Avebury Circle

I see the white clouds blow
From cottages thick-thatched with snow
More clearly than I read
This great stone monster without feet, wings, head:

A huge night-blackening shadow
Set up by kings in this holy meadow,
Where of his fellows most
With those antique Cimmerians are lost.

I wonder if King Sil
Will rise and ride from Silbury Hill
Where buried with his horse
He sits, a strange invulnerable corse,

And grey wethers that keep
On Clatford Down their lichened sleep
Drive to this ancient fold
And bring again an age of stone and gold.

## *In Burnham Beeches*

Walking among these smooth beech-boles
 With cracks and galls
And beetle-holes
 And ivy trickling in green waterfalls,

I noted carvings on their barks,
 Faint and diffuse
As china-marks
 On Worcester or Old Bow: I wondered whose.

I feared that time had played its part
 With those whose token
Was a twin heart,
 So many hearts the swelling bark had broken.

## Prospect of a Mountain

Though cuckoos call across the kyle
And larks are dancing everywhere
To their thin bagpipe's air,
My thoughts are of the autumn day
I climbed that Quinaig, monstrous pile,
And striding up its slaggy brow
Stood outside time and space;
It looks so empty of me now,
More years than miles away,
The mountain-cairn might mark my burial-place.

## Cornish Flower-Farm

Here where the cliff rises so high
The sea below fills half the sky
And ships hang in mid-air,
Set on the cliff-face, square by square,
Walls of veronica enclose
White gladioli in their neat rows
And blue and golden irises;
But though the walls grow tall as trees,
Some flowers from their quiet quillets pass
To mix with wayside weeds and grass,
Like nuns that from their strict retreats
Go visiting the poor in their plain streets.

## The Revenant

O foolish birds, be dumb,
  And you, jay, stop your mocking laughter;
A revenant I come
  To-day as I might come fifty years after.

Why, birds, I am no stranger,
  For as I cross the copse and back,
I feel a double-ganger,
  Who meets himself at each turn of the track.

A better welcome give
  To one who may have bent and blessed
Your fathers four or five
  Laid in the smooth round hollow of a nest.

Come less than fifty years,
  Owls may have cause to mock at one
Who stalks this wood and wears
  A frosty coat that will not stand the sun.

## Spring Flowers

Now we enjoy the rain,
When at each neighbour's door we hear
'How big primroses are this year'—
Tale we may live to hear again —

And dandelions flood
The orchards as though apple-trees
Dropped in the grass ripe oranges,
Boughs still in pink impatient bud,

When too we cannot choose,
But one foot and the other set
In celandine and violet,
Walking in gold and purple shoes,

Rain that through winter weeks
Splashed on our face and window pane,
And rising in these flowers again
Brightens their eyes and fats their cheeks.

## The Blind Man

Speak of the birds, he lifts a listening finger
And 'chiff-chaff' 'willow-warbler' names each singer,
'Hedge-sparrow' 'robin' 'wren'; he knows their cries,
Though all are nightingales to his blind eyes.

## A Mountain Graveyard

Sheep-fold, I thought — till by the dyke
    I saw it lying deep in dock
And knew he never whistled tyke,
    The herd who folded that quiet flock.

## May Frost

It was the night May robbed September
Killing with frost the apple-bloom,
The sunset sunk to its last ember,
I climbed the dew-webbed combe;
There floating from the earth's round rim
I saw the red sun rise.
At first I only thought 'How soon,'
And then 'Surely I must be dying;
These are death's cobwebs on my eyes
That make the dawn so dim;'
And yet my sight was lying:
The frost had set on fire the full-faced moon.

## The Shepherd's Hut

The smear of blue peat smoke
That staggered on the wind and broke,
The only sign of life,
Where was the shepherd's wife,
Who left those flapping clothes to dry,
Taking no thought for her family?
For, as they bellied out
And limbs took shape and waved about,
I thought, She little knows
That ghosts are trying on her children's clothes.

# A Sussex Ghyll

Primroses thick on its steep floor,
This ghyll deserves a better door
Than an old doubled sack
Flung over the barbed fence's narrow back.

The stream has its own way to come;
And though leaves try to keep it dumb
And even choke it dead,
Like a sick man it lies and sings in bed.

The trees are old; some ivy climbs;
Others like lepers drop their limbs;
But this stream delved the ghyll
Till each bank 'Good-bye' said — a distant hill.

# Sudden Thaw

When day dawned with unusual light,
Hedges in snow stood half their height
And in the white-paved village street
Children were walking without feet.

But now by their own breath kept warm
Muck-heaps are naked at the farm
And even through the shrinking snow
Dead bents and thistles start to grow.

## Lady's Slipper Orchid

Though I know well enough
To hunt the Lady's-Slipper now
Is playing blindman's-buff,
For it was June She put it on
And grey with mist the spiders' lace
Swings in the autumn wind,
Yet through this hill-wood, high and low,
I peer in every place;
Seeking for what I cannot find
I do as I have often done
And shall do while I stay beneath the sun.

## In Breckland

Why is it when I cross the warren,
That last year's thistles make more barren,
Rabbits standing upright like men
Dive in their holes again,
And turtle that to turtle purrs
Rises and swerves from the blue belt of firs,
And even the mole that works beneath
Like a small earthquake holds its breath?
Hated by all for other's sins
I bless this rat that only grins,
Stayed by the stiff indifference of death.


## The Haystack

Too dense to have a door,
Window or fireplace or a floor,
They saw this cottage up,
Huge bricks of grass, clover and buttercup
Carting to byre and stable,
Where cow and horse will eat wall, roof and gable.


## The Mud

This glistening mud that loves a gate
Was mashed by cows of late,
But now its puddles lie so still
They hold the clouds and trees and hill;
But when the painted cows come out
From milking-shed to grass
And churn the mud up as they pass,
How cloud and tree and hill will dart about!

*Field-Glasses*

Though buds still speak in hints
And frozen ground has set the flints
As fast as precious stones
And birds perch on the boughs, silent as cones,

Suddenly waked from sloth
Young trees put on a ten year's growth
And stones double their size,
Drawn nearer through field-glasses' greater eyes.

Why I borrow their sight
Is not to give small birds a fright
Creeping up close by inches;
I make the trees come, bringing tits and finches.

I lift a field itself
As lightly as I might a shelf,
And the rooks do not rage
Caught for a moment in my crystal cage.

And while I stand and look,
Their private lives an open book,
I feel so privileged
My shoulders prick, as though they were half-fledged.

## A Dead Bird

Finding the feathers of a bird
Killed by a sparrow-hawk,
I thought, What need is there to walk?
And bound them on my feet;
And as I flew off through the air,
I saw men stare up from a street
And women clasp their hands in prayer.
'To Hades' was no sooner said
Than a winged Hermes I was there;
And though I peered round for the dead,
Nothing I saw and nothing heard
But a low moaning from a bough,
'Ah, who is wearing my poor feathers now?'

## Twilight

As daylight drains away
And darkness creeps out of the wood
And flowers become too faint to tell,
My eyesight failing me as well
And chill dew watering my blood,
I might imagine night was my last day.

But why need I rehearse
What I must play with my whole heart?
Spectators may be moved to tears
To see me act these now-feigned fears;
While others summing up the part
May with approval say, His lines were terse.

## On the Common

The chaffy seeds by the wind blown
Are here so strangely sown,
That one might almost say
The spider's-webs the bushes wear
Have been put down to hay,
And though no crop they bear
Ploughed and cross-ploughed on empty air,
So thick these hay-fields swarm,
That every gorse-bush is become a farm.


## Dundonnel Mountains

Through mist that sets the hills on fire
And rising, never rises higher
Looms a stone figure, gross and squat,
An idol carved out by the weather,
Face, limbs and body lumped together;
And while for none but mountain fox
Eagle or buzzard or wild cat
Its worship may be orthodox,
Death fawning on me from these rocks,
A false step would suffice
To make me both its priest and sacrifice.

## The Beechwood

When the long, varnished buds of beech
Point out beyond their reach,
And tanned by summer suns
Leaves of black bryony turn bronze,
And gossamer floats bright and wet
From trees that are their own sunset,
Spring, summer, autumn I come here,
And what is there to fear?
And yet I never lose the feeling
That someone close behind is stealing
Or else in front has disappeared;
Though nothing I have seen or heard,
The fear of what I might have met
Makes me still walk beneath these boughs
With cautious step as in a haunted house.

## The Dead Sheep

There was a blacksmith in my breast,
That worked the bellows of my chest
  And hammer of my heart,
As up the heavy scree I pressed,
  Making the loose stones scream, crag-echoes start.

Rocks, rising, showed that they were sheep,
But one remained as though asleep,
  And how it was I saw,
When loath to leave the huddled heap
  A hoodie crow rose up with angry craw.

Though stiller than a stone it lay,
The face with skin half-flayed away
  And precious jewels gone,
The eye-pits darted a dark ray
  That searched me to my shadowy skeleton.

## Hard Frost

Frost called to water 'Halt!'
And crusted the moist snow with sparkling salt;
Brooks, their own bridges, stop,
And icicles in long stalactites drop,
And tench in water-holes
Lurk under gluey glass like fish in bowls.

In the hard-rutted lane
At every footstep breaks a brittle pane,
And tinkling trees ice-bound,
Changed into weeping willows, sweep the ground;
Dead boughs take root in ponds
And ferns on windows shoot their ghostly fronds.

But vainly the fierce frost
Interns poor fish, ranks trees in an armed host,
Hangs daggers from house-eaves
And on the windows ferny ambush weaves;
In the long war grown warmer
The sun will strike him dead and strip his armour.

## The Swedes

Three that are one since time began,
Horse, cart and man,
Lurch down the lane patched with loose stones;
Swedes in the cart heaped smooth and round
Like skulls that from the ground
The man has dug without the bones
Leave me in doubt
Whether the swedes with gold shoots sprout
Or with fresh fancies bursts each old bald sconce.

## By the Erme

No trace of absent years
Water or bank or boulder wears;
All is the same as when I went away.

Even my floating face
Seems looking up from the same place,
More steadfast than the stream that cannot stay.

I might have left it there,
Although I notice that my hair
Now stirs a little foam in the smooth bay.

## *View from Mountain*

When through the parting mist,
That the sun's warm gold mouth had kissed,
The hills beneath me came to view
With lochans gleaming here and there,
It was not like the earth I knew;
Another world was shining through,
As though that earth had worn so thin
I saw the living spirit within,
Its beauty almost pain to bear
Waking in me the thought,
If heaven by act of death were brought
Nearer than now, might I not die
Slain by my immortality?

# The Salmon-Leap

Leaves, and not birds, now flit,
Brighter than yellow wagtail and cole-tit,
Or on the water lie
Making a sunset of the fishes' sky.

Autumn for salmon-trout
Is spring, and Io Hymen boulders shout,
Spate drawing them to spawn
Where on high hills the river keeps its dawn.

From rock-lipt lynn to lynn,
Shaking the ferns and grasses with their din,
The cascades overflow
And pour in pools to rise as boiling snow;

Tossing their bodies bare
The salmon-trout are seen tasting our air,
For stronger is the flood
That rages in their few small drops of blood.

## The Rockland Broad

Water too clear to show,
Unless a frown ruffle its brow,
I scarcely feel afloat —
I am suspended in a flying-boat!

Sure, with the land so low
This broad will burst and overflow,
Rush on and never stop,
Till the whole world becomes one water-drop.

Though willow-carrs and reeds
And alders, too, change to seaweeds,
Let Heaven again take note,
Save this new Noah in his flying-boat.


## In the Dingle

As the spring darkened into summer
This dingle rill drew dumber,
Till only sand and gravel
Showed sullen pools the way to travel;
And now no water flows
But what by root and tree-trunk goes,
Sinking and rising up
To bathe a leaf or fill an acorn's cup.

## At Amberley Wild Brooks

Watching the horses stand
And bend their long heads Roman-nosed
With thick cheek veins exposed,
So close to where the brook's bank shelves
They almost meet themselves
In the smooth water sliding by,
I think it strange creatures so great
Can be shut in by wooden gate
And brook no deeper than my hand,
And not like Pegasus shoot wings and fly.

## A Shot Magpie

Though on your long-tailed flight
You wore half-mourning of staid black and white,
So little did the thought of death
Enter your thievish head,
You never knew what choked your breath
When in a day turned night
You fell with feathers heavier than lead.

## By a British Barrow in War-time

Let me lie down beside you, prince,
And share — no, do not wince —
Your grave for a short hour at noon
Shaped, with molehills for stars, like the full moon.

Man in this moon of turf and chalk,
If you can hear me talk
And understand a Saxon stranger,
Listen! to-day our country is in danger.

Does that not stir you, man of bones?
Your country it was once,
Yours when you strode across these downs
Where walls still wave about your hill-top towns.

Or is the news stale in your world
Where hosts are hourly hurled?
Perhaps you learnt from one of these
Who by his death gained a victorious peace.

You do not hear, man in this moon;
The skylarks might as soon
Hear me as you who are not there;
I waste breath that were precious now in prayer.

## At Grime's Graves

These flints that on the warren lie
And glint in moonlight like a snake's eye,
Though chipped by knappers for flint arrows
That flew away like sparrows,
Are still so fresh that one might say
Those dead men were on holiday;
'Few poems keep as fresh as flints,'
The green-eyed moonlight hints;
'Yours will not last as long;
They will not even go for an old song.'


## July

Darker the track to-day
Than any cloudy March or April day
  When nesting birds sang louder,
For hazels hazels, elders elders meet,
Tangle and trip the sun's pale dancing feet
  That beat it to white powder.

That day in January,
I climbed the hill to this wood's sanctuary,
  The track was plain enough;
Now bryony crowds its stars yellow as honey
And close against my face hemp-agrimony
  Pushes its purple faces.

But I may find again
When autumn's fires sink under winter's rain
  A clearer way to pass,
As when that sun with a wan ray of hope
Striking a hollow on the frost furred slope
  Wet one green patch of grass.

# Hymn

Lord, by whose breath all souls and seeds are living
   With life that is and life that is to be,
First-fruits of earth we offer with thanksgiving
   For fields in flood with summer's golden sea.

Lord of the earth, accept these gifts in token
   Thou in thy works are to be all-adored,
From whom the light as daily bread is broken,
   Sunset and dawn as wine and milk are poured.

Poor is our praise, but these shall be our psalter;
   Lo, like thyself they rose up from the dead;
Lord, give them back when at thy holy altar
   We feed on thee, who are the living bread.

# Index of first lines

218